Insights You Need from
Harvard Business Review

THE YEAR IN TECH 2021

Insights You Need from Harvard Business Review

Business is changing. Will you adapt or be left behind?

Get up to speed and deepen your understanding of the topics that are shaping your company's future with the **Insights You Need from Harvard Business Review** series. Featuring HBR's smartest thinking on fast-moving issues—blockchain, cybersecurity, AI, and more—each book provides the foundational introduction and practical case studies your organization needs to compete today and collects the best research, interviews, and analysis to get it ready for tomorrow.

You can't afford to ignore how these issues will transform the landscape of business and society. The Insights You Need series will help you grasp these critical ideas—and prepare you and your company for the future.

Books in the series includes:

Agile

Artificial Intelligence

Blockchain

Climate Change

Coronavirus: Leadership and Recovery

Customer Data and Privacy

Cybersecurity

Monopolies and Tech Giants

Strategic Analytics

The Year in Tech 2021

Insights You Need from
**Harvard
Business
Review**

THE YEAR
IN TECH 2021

Harvard Business Review Press
Boston, Massachusetts

Copyright 2020 Harvard Business School Publishing Corporation
All rights reserved
Printed in the United States of America

10 9 8 7 6 5 4 3 2 1

The web addresses referenced in this book were live and correct at the time of the book's publication but may be subject to change.

Cataloging-in-Publication data is forthcoming.

ISBN: 978-1-63369-907-6
eISBN: 978-1-63369-908-3

The paper used in this publication meets the requirements of the American National Standard for Permanence of Paper for Publications and Documents in Libraries and Archives Z39.48-1992.

Contents

Contents

Section 4

Big Tech, Big Problems

Contents

Introduction

EMBRACING THE CHAOS OF LIFE, WORK, AND MARKETS

by David Weinberger

The articles in this collection look forward from where we are. Grounded in current realities, they point to technologies that business leaders and managers need to be considering now to see how they might be useful, threatening, or perhaps transformative.

But imagine instead that we are looking backward at today from some distant-future vantage point. In this light, these articles also reveal to us how we're thinking about technology these days.

The most obvious point is that when businesses think about technology today, they're usually thinking about digital, connected technology first—AI, blockchain, 5G, connected products—and not about, say, the remarkable advances in genetics, medicine, energy, and—we hope—climate engineering that are likely to transform our lives in the coming years. That's surely not because those disciplines are less important than the digital realm. Rather, our current focus points to some fundamental facts about business. To start, it reminds us that the work companies do is relational and connective. It is about people collaborating to offer products and services, about reaching customers and users, and about the way those users then interact with the business and other users. That's true of virtually all companies, whether based in technology or not.

The overwhelming importance of the type of digital connected technology we now take for granted also makes clear the extent to which businesses have come to embrace the chaos of life, work, and markets. Back in the old days, we thought we could reduce our business practices to relatively simple maps of processes, and we were confident we could manage and control our potential customers by managing and controlling the information we gave them. Now that anyone can connect with anyone else, it's become manifest that if you look closely enough, everything is an exception because everyone is a unique individual and every circumstance is new. In practice, this means that it will always remain a mystery why last week readers clicked on your ad with the yellow background 2% more than the ad with the green one.

That perhaps explains why the word *disrupt* makes so many appearances in this book decades after the Internet first rumbled and then exploded into the world: Disruption continues to be an accurate description of the way we move forward these days, for the Internet has disrupted not only our old ways of doing things, but even our idea of how progress works.

Now AI—especially machine learning—is beginning to reveal our world in a new way. Machine learning systems generate models from data that are as complex as they need to be in order to produce accurate results. These models don't suffer from the human need to reduce complicated situations to a handful of broad strokes of causality and influence that we can understand and rely on. Instead, businesses are learning that they can gain solid benefits by allowing the machines to go hog wild in discerning complex data correlations. This is enabling businesses to see more clearly, and to acknowledge more thoroughly, the messy chaos in which we all live.

We used to think that progress was a relatively low slope headed up a long mountain, with occasional steep steps marking an invention of consequence. But overall, progress was slow, steady, and incremental. Now, as the articles in this book show, progress is about blowing up the entire slope and the mountain it climbs.

"AI is disrupting every industry," says Kane Simms before focusing on the particular AI-enabled technology promised in the article's title, "How Voice Assistants Could Change the Way We Shop." "Artificial intelligence has disrupted every area of our lives," say Tomas Chamorro-Premuzic, Frida Polli, and Ben Dattner in "Building Ethical AI for Talent Management." In "5G's Potential, and Why Businesses Should Start Preparing for It," Omar Abbosh and Larry Downes point to 5G connectivity as an enabler of disruption, a "revolutionary technology" that will "make possible the kind of disruptive applications that usually leave both investors and users salivating." David Furlonger and Christophe Uzureau, in "The Five Kinds of Blockchain Projects (and Which to Watch Out For)," maintain that blockchain technology could pack a disruptive punch to some of the largest institutions in the world and the trust relations they're based on.

All these authors understand that with great disruption comes great risk. For example, the title of Bhaskar Chakravorti's contribution asserts an issue—"Why It's So Hard for Users to Control Their Data"—the premise of which is that our privacy is challenged by our new technology. Stuart Madnick addresses a particularly frightening danger in "How to Safeguard Against Cyberattacks on Utilities." Sara Wilson's concerns are also obvious in the title of her article—"The Era of Antisocial Social Media"—which then lays out a panoply of ways businesses can help stitch the social fabric together.

Even articles that are overall enthusiastic about the tech they are discussing point to sobering issues. Lauren Golembiewski in "How Wearable AI Will Amplify Human Intelligence" wonders about the displacement of human jobs by digital automation. Rather than overhyping the latest tech, Darrell Rigby, Mikey Vu, and Asit Goel tell us in "Four Questions Retailers Need to Ask About Augmented Reality" that AR may promise more than it eventually delivers.

But one concern comes up over and over: how to maintain our humanity as the digital environment increasingly wires itself into our nervous systems. The authors of "Building Ethical AI for Talent Management" advise us to invest in the human expertise that is uniquely able to spot and cultivate talent. In "Learning to Work with Intelligent Machines," Matt Beane points to the *shadow learning* engaged in by employees who are so determined not to be deskilled by our new technology that they're willing to break the rules . . . for which the author salutes them.

None of the authors of these articles let their interest in technology overwhelm their interest in humans. In "Can Biometrics Predict a Viral Marketing Campaign?," Jacob Jones, Matthew Gillespie, and Kelsey Libert remind us that virality is not a property of the content that goes viral but is due to the response human beings have to it. Thales Teixeira in "A Survival Guide for Startups in the Era of Tech Giants" points to great and compassionate customer service as a potent competitive advantage. Lauren Golembiewski in her article on wearable AI sees this technology as an amplifier of human intelligence, enabling us to do jobs that robots can't . . . at least for now. Bhaskar Chakravorti's piece on the user control of data begins by asking companies to grant their users *digital agency* in order to engender a respect for human agency itself. Sarah Wilson, when looking for ways to overcome the antisocial nature of too many social networking technologies, emphasizes the importance of human intimacy for our work lives as well as in our personal lives and finds ways to achieve that with digital media.

These concerns about maintaining our human values arise because we recognize that while we build our machines for our purposes, and we ultimately control them, our relationship with them is far more complex. Ask musicians where their hands end and where their instruments begin . . . and where the music comes from. As the philosopher Martin Heidegger wrote in the early 1950s, "Technology discloses the world"—it reveals the world in one aspect or another. The Internet revealed it as connected, linked, without boundaries, and full of differences. Now machine learning is disclosing a world made of particularities, each affecting everything else at the same time. A world containing hidden signs and signals. A world that is far beyond our capacity to fully understand or predict.

The articles in this collection will guide you toward some of the most important technologies and questions now at hand or coming toward us quickly. They each address one aspect of an intertwined whole that is bigger than we can imagine and that is both frightening and immensely hopeful.

In this, as much as in their insights into their particular topics, they reflect the current state of our world.

Section 1

NEW TECH AND THE EVOLVING CONSUMER EXPERIENCE

1

HOW VOICE ASSISTANTS COULD CHANGE THE WAY WE SHOP

by Kane Simms

AI is disrupting every industry, leading to new business models, further digital transformation, and a future of technology that's more integrated into our natural environment. Smart speakers are the fastest-growing consumer technology since the smartphone, and they are poised to revolutionize the way we interact with technology. Computers can finally speak our language.

A key question for business leaders to consider right now is: How will the voice assistant movement affect the way your customers shop—and how will you, in turn, need to adapt in terms of how to market and sell your products and services?

Strategy consultants OC&C predict that voice shopping will grow to $40 billion–plus in 2022, up from about $2 billion as of this writing, across the United States and the United Kingdom.[1] Some predict even faster growth: Juniper anticipates that number to be $80 billion by 2023.[2]

While early numbers sound promising, you should take them with a grain of salt. Amazon hasn't shared any hard voice shopping numbers, yet reports from The Information in 2019 found that only 2% of Amazon Echo owners have ever tried voice shopping.

It all really depends on how you define *shopping*. In 2018, Voicebot found that one in five U.S. adults had used voice as part of their shopping journey, which could be any point on the path to purchase, not just the transaction itself.[3] In the following year, Voicebot also found that more than 40% of smart speaker users in the United States have searched for a product on a smart speaker.[4]

The general consensus is that voice shopping activities are increasing, but what makes voice shopping itself appealing?

There are a few fundamental reasons why voice shopping has huge potential. If we can understand these reasons, we can shape a strategy that matches or exceeds customer expectations, as more and more consumers use voice assistants to buy goods and services:

It's faster. We can speak faster than we can type, so using voice is typically quicker than any other modality. For example, in 2018, Virgin Trains in the UK launched an Alexa skill that lets customers book train tickets through Alexa. It takes the average booking time down from seven minutes online to two minutes via voice. The potential to save time is always appealing to customers.

It's frictionless. No matter how user friendly you make your website or app, no matter how much you work on your conversion rate, you're always battling the inherent friction that's built into the device itself. Consider that in order to get to your fantastically optimized app, a user has to:

1. Pull out their phone

2. Unlock it

3. Swipe to find your app

4. Tap to open it

5. Wait for it to load

Only then can they begin that delightful experience you've prepared for them. With voice, everything is just an utterance away. There are simply fewer barriers to overcome in order to start the shopping experience.

It can convert leads to sales. It's not just access and speed that are driving the growth of voice shopping. Above all else, voice converts leads into actual sales. Consider the example of Invoked Apps' suite of Alexa skills, which allow users to play ambient sounds, such as white noise, city soundscapes, thunderstorms, and much more. They're some of the most popular Alexa skills in the Skills Store, attracting more than 150,000 users per day.[5] Founder Nick Schwab told me that when Amazon released in-skill purchases (ISPs) for Alexa in 2018, giving developers the ability to sell digital goods through their Alexa skills, Schwab rolled out ISPs in his own skills. This gave users the ability to pay for premium features—namely, to play two different ambient sounds at the same time, such as a city soundscape with an open fire.

When asked about the conversion rate of users upgrading to paid sounds, Schwab said, "Overall I'm seeing around a 3% conversion for users . . . And then the conversion rate from trial to paid is more like 90%, which is staggering."

And voice doesn't just help drive sales of digital goods, such as one-off extra lives in games and subscriptions to premium content; it can lead to increased physical sales, such as train tickets and groceries, and it's even being used in-store to sell products.

The second example of how voice is increasing conversions comes from The Mars Agency. It's trialing an in-store voice assistant called SmartAisle with retailer BevMo!, which helps customers decide which whisky to buy. Here's how it works: An Amazon Echo is installed on an illuminated shelving unit in the whisky aisle in-store. Customers stand in front of the Echo and talk out loud to the SmartAisle skill. In turn, the Echo responds with information about certain types of whisky and guides the customer through a decision-making process. The shelving unit has lights under each bottle, and as the conversation progresses and the assistant begins whittling down the selection, the lights under the ruled-out whiskies dim. At the end of the experience, the customer is left with one whisky bottle illuminated on the shelf. Bree Glaeser, Director of Innovation at The Mars Agency, told me: "People don't always want to go with the opinion of the store clerk."

SmartAisle not only engages customers in-store, but above all else, it actually converts browsers to buyers. Brooke Hawkins, Senior Voice User Interface Designer at The Mars Agency, said: "We're definitely consistently seeing sales lift in the stores that SmartAisle is deployed in."

The Shopping Mall of the Future

The rise of smart speakers with screens could open the door for voice shopping to actually become what it's forecast to be. Devices like the Echo Show and Google Home Nest Hub are the beginning of the multimodal voice experience, where you can see a screen and control it with your voice. Extend this to the Fire TV Stick with Alexa onboard, and the TV could easily become the shopping mall of the future.

Voice is also being extended into the web by companies like Voysis. Rather than wasting time with filtering and searching on a retailer's website, customers using Voysis can just ask for "a pair of red men's Nike trainers under $100 in a size 9," and Voysis will do the filtering for you.

Then there's the emerging use case of the car. Being able to shop for groceries or order takeout from the car creates a completely new environment where people will be able to shop. With almost all major car manufacturers, including Mercedes, BMW, Tesla, and Ford, shipping new motors with in-car voice assistants, and devices like the Alexa Auto equipping older vehicles with a voice assistant, you'll soon be able to order those flowers you forgot for Mother's Day, place a bet on the big game, or impulsively purchase an audiobook to listen to on your way home, all from within your vehicle and all without taking your eyes off the road.

Whether or not you believe the hype of the forecasted numbers, there is simply too much traction and potential with voice shopping for it not to be something that can seriously impact your business. With that said, it doesn't come without its own challenges.

First, there are challenges for retailers, including:

- **Data ownership.** If you choose to use one of the top two platforms, Alexa or Google Assistant, then they'll ultimately have visibility into all of your skill or action activity, including what your users are asking for and buying. That's pretty compelling competitive intelligence.

- **Commission.** For a truly seamless experience, you'll need to use a native payment service, like Amazon Pay or Google Pay. For that, there's a charge.

- **Competition.** Amazon's aim is to be the place where you can buy anything online. That means that whether or not you compete with Amazon today, you might tomorrow. As Joshua Montgomery, CEO of Mycroft told me, "If you're in business, you're probably going to compete with Amazon someday." With that said, how Amazon treats competing products on Alexa is yet to be seen.

Second, there are challenges for consumers, including:

- **Difficulty browsing.** Although we can speak faster than we can type, it's quicker to scan a list of search results than it is to listen to those results read back. This means that general browsing, a common product research behavior, is a challenge on voice.

- **Difficulty discovering possibilities.** Discovering voice applications is a challenge. So finding out what shopping facilities exist on voice and understanding how to access them can be a challenge for some.

- **Cognitive load.** There's also a cognitive load placed on the user in order to access a third-party experience. For example, having to say, "Alexa, ask [brand] to [do something]," relies on the user knowing (a) that the brand exists on the platform and (b) that the brand provides the option for you to do that something.

So, how should companies be preparing for voice shopping? When preparing a voice strategy, the first thing to understand is that voice is more than the two big platforms, Alexa and Google Assistant. Voice is an interface to technology. Your ultimate goal, then, should be for a voice interface to overlay all of your customer touch points, from smart speakers and voice assistants to your website, apps, phone lines, and even in-store experiences. For this, you'll need to develop your skills and understanding of voice user interface (VUI) design practices so that you can match a user's context and needs with your solution.

As with a website or app, a great front end is rarely useful unless it's connected to a smart back end, and this is where voice excels. As part of your voice strategy, the front end should be integrated with your current line of business systems to take advantage of the intelligence you already have. This will enable you to surface products, pricing, stock levels, and previous purchases and give you a basis for processing transactions and answering product-related questions.

By integrating voice with your business systems, voice becomes something that can push your business forward, rather than becoming just a shiny new gimmick. And once you've established the basics of product ordering and research, you'll then be in a position to dig deeper into things like personalization, recommendations, and using the data you've gathered to improve or even create new product lines or content based on what your customers are actively asking you for.

Making voice an integral part of your business won't happen overnight, but businesses that put the wheels in motion now can be out in front in a year's time. But first, you need to get off the starting blocks.

TAKEAWAYS

Smart speakers are the fastest-growing consumer technology since the smartphone. Voice assistants will transform the way customers shop—assess how to market and sell your products and services accordingly.

✓ Voice shopping has huge potential because it's faster (we can speak faster than we type), there's low friction to start a shopping experience (no need to unlock your phone and dig through apps before getting to your site), and it can convert leads to sales at a high rate.

✓ Businesses should look to develop a voice interface to overlay all customer touch points. To begin, integrate your voice strategy with your current line of business systems, and build a basis for surfacing products, processing transactions, and answering product-related questions.

✓ Once you've established the basics, you'll be in a position to dig deeper into personalization, recommendations, and using the data you've gathered to improve or even create new product lines or content.

NOTES

1. Sara Perez, "Voice Shopping Estimated to Hit $40+ Billion Across US and UK by 2022," TechCrunch.com, March 2, 2018, https://techcrunch.com/2018/03/02/voice-shopping-estimated-to-hit-40-billion-across-u-s-and-u-k-by-2022/.

2. Bret Kinsella, "Juniper Forecasts $80 Billion in Voice Commerce in 2023, or $10 Per Assistant," voicebot.ai, February 19, 2019, https://voicebot.ai/2019/02/19/juniper-forecasts-80-billion-in-voice-commerce-in-2023-or-10-per-assistant/.

3. Bret Kinsella and Ava Mutchler, "Voice Shopping Consumer Adoption Report, 2018," voicebot.ai, https://voicebot.ai/voice-shopping-report-2018/.

4. Bret Kinsella and Ava Mutchler, "U.S. Smart Speaker Consumer Adoption Report, 2019," voicebot.ai, https://voicebot.ai/smart-speaker-consumer-adoption-report-2019/.

5. "Adoption, Growth, In-Skill Purchases, and Developer Rewards with Nick Schwab," VUX World podcast, August 18, 2018, https://podcasts.apple.com/gb/podcast/adoption-growth-in-skill-purchases-developer-rewards/id1347820660?i=1000417400729.

Adapted from "How Voice Assistants Could Change the Way We Shop," on hbr.org, May 15, 2019 (product #H04YEN).

AR = augmented reality.

FOUR QUESTIONS RETAILERS NEED TO ASK ABOUT AUGMENTED REALITY

by Darrell K. Rigby, Mikey Vu, and Asit Goel

W hether they are shopping for spectacles or a sofa, consumers have no shortage of augmented reality apps to assist them these days. Following the viral success of Pokémon Go in 2016, hordes of retailers have embraced the technology.

Nintendo's cellphone-enabled treasure hunt was the first big showcase for AR's innovative blend of real-world and computer-generated images. Now the retail sector is using AR to sell items as diverse as furniture, cosmetics, home improvement products, and fashion.

Executives like the way that AR could help make online shopping feel as good as—or better than—shopping in person. Sephora's app does this brilliantly, for instance, by allowing consumers to use their phone cameras to "try on" makeup virtually. Retail leaders also reckon AR will make their physical stores more engaging—and their salespeople more productive.

But AR's promise doesn't make it a great investment for every retailer. Executives must make painful trade-offs among myriad investment options, and they have reason to be suspicious of tempting gadgets. Bets on the likes of 3-D TVs, scan-and-go checkouts, and facial-recognition software have tested their patience. Such innovations may not prove worthless, but they are certainly worth less than tech dreamers imagined.

The recent collapse and relaunch of Blippar, a prominent European AR startup that created AR apps for consumer goods and retail customers such as Covent Garden, Net-a-Porter, and McDonald's, have added to worries that, for all its promise, AR might struggle to reach the mainstream. Forrester recently reported that new venture capital funding for AR in 2018 was $1.69 billion, less than half the $3.58 billion raised in 2017.[1] "We believe such a dramatic pull-back is in direct response to expensive and underwhelming results from early adopters of [AR and VR]," Forrester said, advising companies considering AR to "proceed with an abundance of caution."

So, how should retailers determine the appropriate role for AR in their businesses? By answering four questions that could apply to almost any technology decision.

Will our customers value this (more than a price cut)? Customers have a hard time telling us what they will want. We haven't met any customers who were asking for Pokémon Go. Conventional wisdom says that clothing shoppers want fashion advice, top-notch service, and experiential ambience, yet we watch Amazon and discounters such as T.J. Maxx gain market share with lower prices (and a "root through the piles" treasure hunt at the latter's stores).

Whether retailers make or buy them, AR apps cost real money—anywhere from $300,000 to $30 million for development costs alone. Are customers willing to pay for that, or would they rather have lower prices? The answer depends on whether your targets are aggressive adopters of technology, the app enhances your brand, and the purchase and usage of your product is sufficiently complex to justify the use of AR.

Furniture apps such as Ikea Place use AR to ease a notorious source of pain for shoppers—namely, the difficulty of predicting what a couch, bed, or table will look like when brought home. Will it fit into the available space? Will it go with the existing furniture, carpets, and walls? That's a perfect problem for AR to solve. Consumers really suffer when they buy the wrong furniture online: They might lose eight weeks waiting for delivery only then to be forced into the nightmare that engulfs those trying to return these bulky items. The value to the consumer is high relative to the cost of the innovation.

Does the technology have value to a wide range of customers? When you're thinking about AR's value to customers, don't stop with consumers. It turns out that AR can be useful in education and training simulations, helping field representatives perform maintenance and repairs and testing complex store designs and tricky user experiences.

Often these uses are more profitable than consumer apps and are the right places to begin building AR capabilities. For instance, stock pickers at a Dutch e-commerce warehouse operator worked 15% faster when they were equipped with Google Glass; orders were pushed directly to the AR-enabled spectacles, accelerating a process that had relied on the retrieval of physical printouts.[2] Start with the most profitable applications and move on to the tougher ones.

Can the math work? Even if the math turns out to be wrong, it's worth laying out how a technology such as AR is supposed to improve profits. Is it supposed to improve sales (the number of customers who visit each year, the frequency of shopping visits per year, the percentage of shopping visits that create purchases, the number of categories shopped, the number of items purchased per category, the average unit revenue per item)? Is it supposed to reduce costs (labor, materials, distribution, marketing)? Is it supposed to reduce inventory levels or capital expenses?

Limit the intangible benefits. Don't just "imagine the PR power"; quantify the improvement in marketing expenses. With these kinds of estimates in hand, it is far easier to test initial assumptions, compare actual results with early estimates, improve investment proposals over time, and identify better ways of solving customer problems.

And don't forget to look for creative sources of funding. Technology vendors often are willing to subsidize AR projects for learning and publicity purposes. Merchandise vendors may be willing to pay to have their products featured in the apps.

Where does this belong on our technology backlog? Let's face it: The technology systems of most retailers are dreadful. As a result, they become the choking points for almost every important innovation that retailers need to succeed. Yet the number of projects heaped onto this creaking infrastructure is growing fast. This is why the biggest question of all is how you should prioritize and sequence AR on your technology to-do list.

Given constraints on budgets and the hiring of tech experts, the results are often disastrous when retail executives add projects to this to-do list. Delays ripple across the existing backlog. Meanwhile, customer needs evolve, and nimbler competitors charge ahead, making many of these stalled projects obsolete.

Retail executives can't see technology projects piling up the way they can see inventory stacked in warehouses or backrooms. But technology projects are every bit as expensive and perishable as physical inventories. Retailers need to stop starting innovation projects and start finishing them.

Agile methods often sequence technology projects according to their cost of delay. In other words, what would it cost to delay this project by one month? These costs can be a matter of life and death for core technology projects in retail such as e-commerce websites and apps, the integration of online and off-line shopping, advanced analytics, and call center improvements.

And the costs of delaying an AR project? Let's just say that we haven't seen any retailers die because their AR project was delayed by a year. Nor have we seen languishing retailers leap to leadership based on their AR apps.

As a tool, AR likely will get more powerful. It helps that billions of people will always have an AR-enabled gadget in their pocket or handbag. But the appropriate role for it will vary significantly by retail sector and by the health of a retailer's core technologies. So while AR should be on many retailers' test-and-learn lists, it should not delay the advancement and completion of more important tech projects that will determine whether these companies follow the path of Amazon or that of Toys "R" Us.

TAKEAWAYS

There is no shortage of augmented reality apps in the marketplace to assist consumers in purchasing items ranging from furniture to cosmetics. But AR's potential doesn't make it a great investment for every retailer. To determine whether AR should have a role in your businesses, answer these four questions:

- ✓ Will our customers value an AR experience (more than a price cut)? AR apps are expensive to build. Are your customers willing to pay more for AR features, or would they prefer lower prices?

✓ Does the technology have value to a wide range of customers? When considering AR's value, don't stop with consumers—it can be useful in education, training simulations, and many other areas.

✓ Can the math work? Build a business case for how AR is supposed to improve profits. Will it improve sales, reduce costs, reduce inventory levels, or reduce capital expenses?

✓ Where does this belong on our technology backlog? AR should not delay the advancement and completion of more critical tech projects.

NOTES

1. Carlton Doty, "New Tech Spotlight: Let's Get Real About Extended Reality," Forrester.com, February 4, 2019, https://go .forrester.com/blogs/new-tech-spotlight-lets-get-real-about -extended-reality/.

2. Jeroen Dekker, "Active Ants gebruikt als eerste in Nederland Google Glass voor orderpicking," Active Ants blog, May 7, 2018, https://www.activeants.nl/blog/active-ants-google-glass/.

Adapted from "Four Questions Retailers Need to Ask About Augmented Reality," on hbr.org, April 18, 2019 (product #H04WK6).

Section 2

WORKING BETTER WITH ADVANCED TECHNOLOGIES

BUILDING ETHICAL AI FOR TALENT MANAGEMENT

by Tomas Chamorro-Premuzic, Frida Polli, and Ben Dattner

A rtificial intelligence has disrupted every area of our lives—from the curated shopping experiences we've come to expect from companies like Amazon and Alibaba to the personalized recommendations that channels like YouTube and Netflix use to market their latest content. But when it comes to the workplace, in many ways, AI is still in its infancy. This is particularly true when we consider the ways it is beginning to change talent management. To use a familiar analogy: AI at work is in the dial-up mode. The 5G Wi-Fi phase has yet to arrive, but we have no doubt that it will.

To be sure, there is much confusion around what AI can and cannot do, as well as different perspectives on how to define it. In the war for talent, however, AI plays a very specific role: to give organizations more accurate and more efficient predictions of a candidate's work-related behaviors and performance potential. Unlike traditional recruitment methods, such as employee referrals, CV screening, and face-to-face interviews, AI is able to find patterns unseen by the human eye.

Many AI systems use real people as models for what success looks like in certain roles. This group of individuals is referred to as a *training data set* and often includes managers or staff who have been defined as *high performers*. AI systems process and compare the profiles of various job applicants to the "model" employee it has created based on the training set. Then, it gives the company a probabilistic estimate of how closely a candidate's attributes match those of the ideal employee.

Theoretically, this method could be used to find the right person for the right role faster and more efficiently than ever before. But, as you may have realized, it has become a source of both promise and peril. If the training set is diverse, if demographically unbiased data is used to measure the people in it, and if the algorithms are also debiased, this technique can actually mitigate human prejudice and expand diversity and socioeconomic inclusion better than humans ever could. However, if the training set, the data, or both are biased, and algorithms are not sufficiently audited, AI will only exacerbate the problem of bias in hiring and homogeneity in organizations.

In order to rapidly improve talent management and take full advantage of the power and potential AI offers, then, we need to shift our focus from developing more ethical HR systems to developing more ethical AI. Of course, removing bias from AI is not easy. In fact, it is very hard. But our argument is based on our belief that it is far more feasible than removing it from humans themselves.

When it comes to identifying talent or potential, most organizations still play it by ear. Recruiters spend just a few seconds looking at a résumé before deciding who to "weed out." Hiring managers make quick judgments and call them "intuition" or overlook hard data and hire based on cultural fit—a problem made worse by the general absence of objective and rigorous performance measures. Further, the unconscious bias training implemented by a growing number of companies has often been found to be ineffective and, at times, can even make things worse. Often, training focuses too much on individual bias and too little on the structural biases narrowing the pipeline of underrepresented groups.

Though critics argue that AI is not much better, they often forget that these systems are mirroring our own behavior. We are quick to blame AI for predicting that white men will receive higher performance ratings from their (probably also white male) managers. But this is happening because we have failed to fix bias in the performance ratings that are often used in training data sets. We are shocked that AI can make biased hiring decisions but are fine living in a world where human biases dominate them. Just take a look at Amazon. The outcry of criticism about their biased recruiting algorithm ignored the overwhelming evidence that current human-driven hiring in most organizations is ineradicably worse. It's akin to expressing more concern over a very small number of driverless car deaths than the 1.2 million traffic deaths a year caused by flawed and possibly also distracted or intoxicated humans.

Realistically, we have a greater ability to ensure both accuracy and fairness in AI systems than we do to influence or enlighten recruiters and hiring managers. Humans are very good at learning but very bad at unlearning. The cognitive mechanisms that make us biased are often the same tools we use to survive in our day-to-day lives. The world is far too complex for us to process logically and deliberately all the time; if we did, we would be overwhelmed by information overload and unable to make simple decisions, such as buying a cup of coffee (after all, why should we trust the barista if we don't know him?). That's why it's easier to ensure that our data and training sets are unbiased than it is to change the behaviors of Sam or Sally, from whom we can neither remove bias nor extract a printout of the variables that influence their decisions. Essentially, it is easier to unpack AI algorithms than to understand and change the human mind.

To do this, organizations using AI for talent management, at any stage, should start by taking the following steps.

1. Educate candidates and obtain their consent. Ask prospective employees to opt in or to provide their personal data to the company, knowing that it will be analyzed, stored, and used by AI systems for making HR-related decisions. Be ready to explain the *what*, *who*, *how*, and *why*. It's not ethical for AI systems to rely on black-box models. If a candidate has an attribute that is associated with success in a role, the organization needs to not only understand why that is the case but also be able to explain the causal links. In short, AI systems should be designed to predict and explain "causation," not just find "correlation." You should also be sure to preserve candidate anonymity to protect personal data and comply with the General Data Protection Regulation (GDPR), California privacy laws, and similar regulations.

2. Invest in systems that optimize for fairness *and* accuracy. Historically, organizational psychologists have pointed to a drop in accuracy when candidate assessments are optimized for fairness. For example, much academic research indicates that while cognitive ability tests are a consistent predictor of job performance, particularly in high-complexity jobs, their deployment has adverse impact on underrepresented groups, particularly individuals with a lower socioeconomic status. This means that companies interested in boosting diversity and creating an inclusive culture often de-emphasize traditional cognitive tests when hiring new workers so that diverse candidates are not disadvantaged in the process. This is known as the fairness/accuracy trade-off.

However, this trade-off is based on techniques from half a century ago, prior to the advent of AI models that can treat the data very differently than traditional models. There is increasing evidence that AI could overcome this trade-off by deploying more dynamic and personalized scoring algorithms that are sensitive as much to accuracy as to fairness, optimizing for a mix of both. Therefore, developers of AI have no excuse for not doing so. Further, because these new systems now exist, we should question whether the widespread use of traditional cognitive assessments, which are known to have an adverse impact on minorities, should continue without some form of bias mitigation.

3. Develop open-source systems and third-party audits. Hold companies and developers accountable by allowing others to audit the tools being used to analyze their applications. One solution is open sourcing nonproprietary yet critical aspects of the AI technology the organization uses. For proprietary components, third-party audits conducted by credible experts in the field are a tool companies can use to show the public how they are mitigating bias.

4. Follow the same laws—as well as data collection and usage practices—used in traditional hiring. Any data that shouldn't be collected or included in a traditional hiring process for legal or ethical reasons should not be used by AI systems. Private information about physical, mental, or emotional conditions, genetic information, and substance use or abuse should never be entered.

If organizations address these issues, we believe that ethical AI could vastly improve organizations not only by reducing bias in hiring but also by enhancing meritocracy and making the association between talent, effort, and employee success far greater than it has been in the past. Further, it will be good for the global economy. Once we mitigate bias, our candidate pools will grow beyond employee referrals and Ivy League graduates. People from a wider range of socioeconomic backgrounds will have more access to better jobs—which can help create balance and begin to remedy class divides.

To make the above happen, however, businesses need to make the right investments, not just in cutting-edge AI technologies but also (and especially) in human expertise— people who understand how to leverage the advantages that these new technologies offer while minimizing potential risks and drawbacks. In any area of performance, a combination of artificial and human intelligence is likely to produce a better result than one without the other. Ethical AI should be viewed as one of the tools we can use to counter our own biases, not as a final panacea.

TAKEAWAYS

AI could give organizations faster, better, and more efficient predictions of a job candidate's behaviors and performance potential. But if the training set, the data, or both are biased, and algorithms are not sufficiently audited, AI will only exacerbate the problems of bias in hiring and homogeneity in organizations. To ensure both accuracy and fairness in AI systems used for talent management, take the following steps:

✓ Focus on creating systems designed to show causation over correlation. If a candidate has an attribute that is associated with success in a role, the AI algorithm needs to be able to explain the links between the two.

✓ Optimize for both fairness and accuracy, instead of one over the other.

✓ Hold your company and developers accountable by allowing third parties to audit your AI tools.

✓ Follow the same laws—as well as data collection and usage practices—you use in traditional hiring.

Adapted from "Building Ethical AI for Talent Management," on hbr.org, November 21, 2019 (product #H05AD9).

THE FIVE KINDS OF BLOCKCHAIN PROJECTS (AND WHICH TO WATCH OUT FOR)

by David Furlonger and Christophe Uzureau

Blockchain burst on the tech scene ten years ago with the launch of Bitcoin. That first introduction led many business leaders to see blockchain and cryptocurrencies as synonymous. In fact, blockchain's value proposition is far broader. At its most basic, it allows two or more people, businesses, or computers to exchange value in digital environments without having an intermediary like a bank or a third-party platform between them. In other words, blockchain redefines the terms of trade for the digital economy.

Consider, for example, how a car insurance blockchain could store policy details and contract rules and automatically process third-party claims, improving efficiency and reducing fraud; or how a hospital blockchain could capture medical records and share them on demand with authorized providers; or how a blockchain could capture the custody trail of French wine all the way back to the vineyard, or diamonds to the mine, reducing counterfeiting.

Each of these solutions already exists, along with scores of others. Despite widespread experimentation, however, blockchain is still young and evolving. Today's experiments often use only some of the core elements that make a blockchain, while rejecting others. In particular, today's blockchains rarely include tokens, and their technology architecture is almost never decentralized, as was intended in the original blockchain design. What that means in practice is that many blockchain solutions available today are owned and governed by a single company or small group, and only authorized participants can join. (The Bitcoin blockchain, in contrast, has no single owner, and anyone who wants to can participate.)

Centralized governance has allowed business leaders to experiment with the technology while sidestepping controversial questions around security, consensus, identity, and anonymity, among others. Yet the centralized model also creates new risks around how the technology, economics, and governance of the blockchain are controlled, particularly as it relates to four business "currencies" produced in digital environments. These currencies are:

1. The **data** about participants and transactions that the solution accesses, collects, and/or generates

2. The **contracts** that define the commercial terms and conditions of participation

3. The **access** to a given market

4. The **technology** from which a blockchain is built

When one company or consortium of companies builds a centralized blockchain, that dominant company can theoretically own the technology, capture and centralize the data, control who can access (or not access) the solution, and set the terms of the contracts.

Of course, not all blockchains have powerful owners, and not all owners want to exert long-term control. Some solutions are highly centralized with one owner or group of owners controlling the currencies, while others exert less absolute control.

To help business leaders identify the difference, we have defined the following five blockchain archetypes based on their degree of centralization.

Archetype 1: Fear of Missing Out Solutions

FOMO solutions are completely centralized, as they are often led by a single company for use in-house or with a very limited set of partners. They usually come about because the company wants to be seen as innovative but hasn't fully considered how the blockchain will add value to the business, or whether it is the best technology for the job. As a result, FOMO projects might be blockchain shoehorned into an existing tech initiative for which the company is ill-suited. Depending on where the order originates, even very senior leaders might feel like they have no choice but to go along. As the CIO of a regional financial services firm told us, "You don't understand; my CEO told me to do blockchain."

Although FOMO blockchain solutions won't create much value, they aren't always pointless. They could send a message to the market that your organization is on top of current trends. Prospective customers might give you a second look. Competitors might invest time and resources for similar FOMO reasons.

Beware, however, of FOMO backlash. When a poorly planned project produces little value, leaders might erroneously conclude that they "tried blockchain" and failed, when they simply had the wrong use case. These solutions could also burden existing systems and processes and create additional costs that bring no increase in efficiency.

Archetype 2: Trojan Horse Solutions

For this archetype, one powerful actor such as a digital giant, a dominant supply-chain participant, or a small group develops a blockchain solution and invites other ecosystem participants to use it. We've dubbed these solutions Trojan horses because they look attractive from the outside. They have a respected brand behind them. They often have strong technological foundations. They usually address known, expensive, and wide-reaching problems in an industry. But they may also require participants to share their company's data and transfer some control or influence in a way that leads to market consolidation for the main blockchain owner.

A food-tracking blockchain is a potential example of a Trojan horse solution. Retailers cite food safety as the rationale for launching it, which makes sense. In the non-blockchain environment, it can take weeks to pinpoint the exact farm or processing plant responsible for a contamination, and dozens of people can fall ill in that time. Complete, accessible records will allow stores to more quickly find the origins of a contamination and stop it at its source. Or, e-commerce companies can improve tracking and tracing of agricultural products and prevent the sale of counterfeit milk, wine, and honey, to name a few.

The risk for the participants on Trojan horse blockchain, however, is that they become dependent on the owner's technology and locked into the contract terms. Over time, the Trojan horse could exert more control over the market as it amasses supply-side data. The business currencies in a Trojan horse archetype would trade at a high risk level for participants.

Archetype 3: Opportunistic Solutions

Opportunistic solutions aim to address known problems or opportunities around record-keeping that are ill-served by existing solutions. Examples include a blockchain solution in development by the Australian Securities Exchange to streamline financial trading. The Depository Trust and Clearing Corporation (DTCC), the post-trade clearing and settlement intermediary for the U.S. financial system, likewise created a blockchain for managing records from credit-default swaps.

Opportunistic experiments can bring value to participants, even if they don't lead to a live, operational platform. The former CIO of a Middle Eastern bank who shared his experience launching a blockchain initiative that was shut down within six months said the experience helped the bank gain confidence in blockchain, while his staff acquired new technology skills. "We got good experience of how it all worked, we spent [very little], and our tech exit strategy maintained the client experience." He added, "It was good PR for the bank!" Opportunistic solutions may present some loss of control over data and contracts. But as the bank CIO acknowledged, the solutions offer experiential payoff.

Archetype 4: Evolutionary Solutions

Blockchain solutions in the evolutionary archetype are designed to mature over time to use tokens with decentralized governance. One example comes from an unlikely source: the Union of European Football Associations (UEFA), the central governing body for European football. UEFA is working with SecuTix and TIXnGO, Swiss technology companies that are part of the Swiss IT company ELCA Group, on an evolutionary solution to drive a safer and more equitable secondary market for football ticket sales.

The platform works by prompting a ticket buyer to download SecuTix's TIXnGO app. The app is connected to a blockchain, and tickets are tokenized so that the platform can record the ticket purchase and link its ownership details. If an owner wants to give a ticket away to a friend or family member, he or she can do that through the app, which sends the record of the transfer to the blockchain. When a ticket holder wants to put the ticket on the open market, the SecuTix platform defines the markup resellers are allowed to charge. This practice prevents price gouging and limits the incentives illegal brokers have to participate.

Over time, the secondary market for tickets could evolve into a decentralized sales network that connects all the secondary ticket sellers in that ecosystem. The business currencies in an evolutionary solution would trade at a low to moderate risk level for participants.

Archetype 5: Blockchain-Native Solutions

Solutions in the fifth and final blockchain archetype are developed either by startups or by innovation arms of existing firms to create a new market or disrupt an existing business model. They may not start out with tokens or decentralized governance, but they are designed to move in that direction as the market matures.

One sector with blockchain-native activity is higher education. Woolf University, founded by a group of academics from Oxford and Cambridge, aspires to be a nonprofit "borderless, digital education society," a decentralized Airbnb for degree courses. Woolf University connects professors with students via secure contracts and captures a record of the learning exchange so that the student can get credit and the professor can get paid.

Gaming also has a burgeoning blockchain community populated by solutions like Enjin, a gaming platform that allows users to create their own tokens to support their games.

Native blockchain solutions will insert new business approaches into legacy industries. Untested technology will be the major currency risk, though these solutions will appeal to participants who want to control their own data and experiment with decentralization.

Blockchain solutions offer alternative ways for businesses to address known challenges involving data sharing and workflows, but buyer beware of giving up too much control over the business currencies of data, technology, access, and contracts. Weigh your options and tolerance for risk, but don't let concerns keep you out of the market. The terms of competition in a digital world are being defined now. The real business of blockchain allows enterprises a chance to win the race.

TAKEAWAYS

As businesses adopt blockchain, they should beware giving up too much control over data, technology, access, and contracts. As you consider projects, you should understand the differences between five blockchain archetypes:

✓ Fear of missing out solutions: FOMO solutions are completely centralized, usually led by a single company for use in-house or with a very limited set of partners. Blockchain often isn't is the best technology for these jobs.

✓ Trojan horse solutions: One powerful actor, such as a digital giant, develops a blockchain solution and invites other ecosystem participants to use it. Participants on these blockchains risk becoming dependent on the owner's technology and locked in.

✓ Opportunistic solutions: These aim to address known problems or opportunities around record-keeping that are ill-served by existing solutions. They can bring value to participants even if they don't lead to a live, operational platform.

✓ Evolutionary solutions: These are designed to take an existing process or solution, tokenize it, and allow it to mature over time from centralized governance to decentralized governance.

✓ Blockchain-native solutions: These are developed either by startups or by innovation arms of existing firms to create new markets or disrupt an existing business model. They are either launched with tokens and decentralized governance or designed to move in that direction as the market matures.

Adapted from The Real Business of Blockchain: How Leaders Can Create Value in a New Digital Age, *by David Furlonger and Christopher Uzureau, Harvard Business Review Press, 2019.*

LEARNING TO WORK WITH INTELLIGENT MACHINES

by Matt Beane

I t's 6:30 in the morning, and Kristen is wheeling her prostate patient into the OR. She's a senior resident, a surgeon in training. Today she's hoping to do some of the procedure's delicate, nerve-sparing dissection herself. The attending physician is by her side, and their four hands are mostly in the patient, with Kristen leading the way under his watchful guidance. The work goes smoothly, the attending backs away, and Kristen closes the patient by 8:15, with a junior resident looking over her shoulder. She lets him do the final line of sutures. She feels great: The patient's going to be fine, and she's a better surgeon than she was at 6:30.

Fast-forward six months. It's 6:30 a.m. again, and Kristen is wheeling another patient into the OR, but this time for robotic prostate surgery. The attending leads the setup of a thousand-pound robot, attaching each of its four arms to the patient. Then he and Kristen take their places at a control console 15 feet away. Their backs are to the patient, and Kristen just watches as the attending remotely manipulates the robot's arms, delicately retracting and dissecting tissue. Using the robot, he can do the entire procedure himself, and he largely does. He knows Kristen needs practice, but he also knows she'd be slower and would make more mistakes. So she'll be lucky if she operates more than 15 minutes during the four-hour surgery. And she knows that if she slips up, he'll tap a touch screen and resume control, very publicly banishing her to watch from the sidelines.

Surgery may be extreme work, but until recently surgeons in training learned their profession the same way most of us learned how to do our jobs: We watched an expert, got involved in the easier work first, and then progressed to harder, often riskier tasks under close supervision until we became experts ourselves. This process goes by lots of names: apprenticeship, mentorship, on-the-job learning (OJL). In surgery it's called *See one, do one, teach one.*

Critical as it is, companies tend to take on-the-job learning for granted; it's almost never formally funded or managed, and little of the estimated $366 billion companies spent globally on formal training in 2018 directly addressed it. Yet decades of research show that although employer-provided training is important, the lion's share of the skills needed to reliably perform a specific job can be learned only by doing it. Most organizations depend heavily on OJL: A 2011 Accenture survey, the most recent of its kind and scale, revealed that only one in five workers had learned any new job skills through formal training in the previous five years.

Today OJL is under threat. The headlong introduction of sophisticated analytics, AI, and robotics into many aspects of work is fundamentally disrupting this time-honored and effective approach. Tens of thousands of people will lose or gain jobs every year as those technologies automate work, and hundreds of millions will have to learn new skills and ways of working. Yet broad evidence demonstrates that companies' deployment of intelligent machines often blocks this critical learning pathway: My colleagues and I have found that it moves trainees away from learning opportunities and experts away from the action, and overloads both with a mandate to master old and new methods simultaneously.

How, then, will employees learn to work alongside these machines? Early indications come from observing learners engaged in norm-challenging practices that are pursued out of the limelight and tolerated for the results they produce. I call this widespread and informal process *shadow learning*.

Obstacles to Learning

My discovery of shadow learning came from two years of watching surgeons and surgical residents at 18 top-rated teaching hospitals in the United States. I studied learning and training in two settings: traditional ("open") surgery and robotic surgery. I gathered data on the challenges robotic surgery presented to senior surgeons, residents, nurses, and scrub technicians (who prep patients, help glove and gown surgeons, pass instruments, and so on), focusing particularly on the few residents who found new, rule-breaking ways to learn. Although this research concentrated on surgery, my broader purpose was to identify learning and training dynamics that would show up in many kinds of work with intelligent machines.

To this end, I connected with a small but growing group of field researchers who are studying how people work with smart machines in settings such as internet start-ups, policing organizations, investment banking, and online education. Their work reveals dynamics like those I observed in surgical training. Drawing on their disparate lines of research, I've identified four widespread obstacles to acquiring needed skills. Those obstacles drive shadow learning.

1. Trainees are being moved away from their "learning edge"

Training people in any kind of work can incur costs and decrease quality, because novices move slowly and make mistakes. As organizations introduce intelligent machines, they often manage this by reducing trainees' participation in the risky and complex portions of the work, as Kristen found. Thus trainees are being kept from situations in which they struggle near the boundaries of their capabilities and recover from mistakes with limited help—a requirement for learning new skills.

The same phenomenon can be seen in investment banking New York University's Callen Anthony found that junior analysts in one firm were increasingly being separated from senior partners as those partners interpreted algorithm-assisted company valuations in M&As. The junior analysts were tasked with simply pulling raw reports from systems that scraped the web for financial data on companies of interest and passing them to the senior partners for analysis. The implicit rationale for this division of labor? First, reduce the risk that junior people would make mistakes in doing sophisticated work close to the customer; and second, maximize senior partners' efficiency: The less time they needed to explain the work to junior staffers, the more they could focus on their higher-level analysis. This provided some short-term gains in efficiency, but it moved junior analysts away from challenging, complex work, making it harder for them to learn the entire valuation process and diminishing the firm's future capability.

2. Experts are being distanced from the work

Sometimes intelligent machines get between trainees and the job, and other times they're deployed in a way that prevents experts from doing important hands-on work. In robotic surgery, surgeons don't see the patient's body or the robot for most of the procedure, so they can't directly assess and manage critical parts of it. For example, in traditional surgery, the surgeon would be acutely aware of how devices and instruments impinged on the patient's body and would adjust accordingly; but in robotic surgery, if a robot's arm hits a patient's head or a scrub is about to swap a robotic instrument, the surgeon won't know unless someone tells her. This has two learning implications: Surgeons can't practice the skills needed to make holistic sense of the work on their own, and they must build new skills related to making sense of the work through others.

Benjamin Shestakofsky, now at the University of Pennsylvania, described a similar phenomenon at a pre-IPO start-up that used machine learning to match local laborers with jobs and that provided a platform for laborers and those hiring them to negotiate terms. At first the algorithms weren't making good matches, so managers in San Francisco hired people in the Philippines to manually create each match. And when laborers had difficulty with the platform—for instance, in using it to issue price quotes to those hiring, or to structure payments—the start-up managers outsourced the needed support to yet another distributed group of employees, in Las Vegas. Given their limited resources, the managers threw bodies at these problems to buy time while they sought the money and additional engineers needed to perfect the product. Delegation allowed the managers and engineers to focus on business development and writing code, but it deprived them of critical learning opportunities: It separated them from direct, regular input from customers—the laborers and the hiring contractors—about the problems they were experiencing and the features they wanted.

3. Learners are expected to master both old and new methods

Robotic surgery comprises a radically new set of techniques and technologies for accomplishing the same ends that traditional surgery seeks to achieve. Promising greater precision and ergonomics, it was simply added to the curriculum, and residents were expected to learn robotic as well as open approaches. But the curriculum didn't include enough time to learn both thoroughly, which often led to a worst-case outcome: The residents mastered neither. I call this problem *methodological overload*.

Shreeharsh Kelkar, at UC Berkeley, found that something similar happened to many professors who were using a new technology platform called edX to develop massive open online courses (MOOCs). EdX provided them with a suite of course-design tools and instructional advice based on fine-grained algorithmic analysis of students' interaction with the platform (clicks, posts, pauses in video replay, and so on). Those who wanted to develop and improve online courses had to learn a host of new skills—how to navigate the edX user interface, interpret analytics on learner behavior, compose and manage the course's project team, and more—while keeping "old school" skills sharp for teaching their traditional classes. Dealing with this tension was difficult for everyone, especially because the approaches were in constant flux: New tools, metrics, and expectations arrived almost daily, and instructors had to quickly assess and master them. The only people who handled both old and new methods well were those who were already technically sophisticated and had significant organizational resources.

4. Standard learning methods are presumed to be effective

Decades of research and tradition hold trainees in medicine to the *See one, do one, teach one* method, but as we've seen, it doesn't adapt well to robotic surgery. Nonetheless, pressure to rely on approved learning methods is so strong that deviation is rare: Surgical-training research, standard routines, policy, and senior surgeons all continue to emphasize traditional approaches to learning, even though the method clearly needs updating for robotic surgery.

Sarah Brayne, at the University of Texas, found a similar mismatch between learning methods and needs among police chiefs and officers in Los Angeles as they tried to apply traditional policing approaches to beat assignments generated by an algorithm. Although the efficacy of such "predictive policing" is unclear, and its ethics are controversial, dozens of police forces are becoming deeply reliant on it. The LAPD's PredPol system breaks the city up into 500-foot squares, or "boxes," assigns a crime probability to each one, and directs officers to those boxes accordingly. Brayne found that it wasn't always obvious to the officers—or to the police chiefs— when and how the former should follow their AI-driven assignments. In policing, the traditional and respected model for acquiring new techniques has been to combine a little formal instruction with lots of old-fashioned learning on the beat. Many chiefs therefore presumed that officers would mostly learn how to incorporate crime forecasts on the job. This dependence on traditional OJL contributed to confusion and resistance to the tool and its guidance. Chiefs didn't want to tell officers what to do once "in the box," because they wanted them to rely on their experiential knowledge and discretion. Nor did they want to irritate the officers by overtly reducing their autonomy and coming across as micromanagers. But by relying on the traditional OJL approach, they inadvertently sabotaged learning: Many officers never understood how to use PredPol or its potential benefits, so they wholly dismissed it—yet they were still held accountable for following its assignments. This wasted time, decreased trust, and led to miscommunication and faulty data entry—all of which undermined their policing.

Shadow Learning Responses

Faced with such barriers, shadow learners are bending or breaking the rules out of view to get the instruction and experience they need. We shouldn't be surprised. Close to a hundred years ago, the sociologist Robert Merton showed that when legitimate means are no longer effective for achieving a valued goal, deviance results. Expertise— perhaps the ultimate occupational goal—is no exception: Given the barriers I've described, we should expect people to find deviant ways to learn key skills. Their approaches are often ingenious and effective, but they can take a personal and an organizational toll: Shadow learners may be punished (for example, by losing practice opportunities and status) or cause waste and even harm. Still, people repeatedly take those risks, because their learning methods work well where approved means fail. It's almost always a bad idea to uncritically copy these deviant practices, but organizations do need to learn from them.

Following are the shadow learning practices that I and others have observed:

Seeking struggle

Recall that robotic surgical trainees often have little time on task. Shadow learners get around this by looking for opportunities to operate near the edge of their capability and with limited supervision. They know they must struggle to learn, and that many attending physicians are unlikely to let them. The subset of residents I studied who did become expert found ways to get the time on the robots they needed. One strategy was to seek collaboration with attendings who weren't themselves seasoned experts. Residents in urology—the specialty having by far the most experience with robots—would rotate into departments whose attendings were less proficient in robotic surgery, allowing the residents to leverage the halo effect of their elite (if limited) training. The attendings were less able to detect quality deviations in their robotic surgical work and knew that the urology residents were being trained by true experts in the practice; thus they were more inclined to let the residents operate, and even to ask for their advice. But few would argue that this is an optimal learning approach.

What about those junior analysts who were cut out of complex valuations? The junior and senior members of one group engaged in shadow learning by disregarding the company's emerging standard practice and working together. Junior analysts continued to pull raw reports to produce the needed input, but they worked alongside senior partners on the analysis that followed.

In some ways this sounds like a risky business move. Indeed, it slowed down the process, and because it required the junior analysts to handle a wider range of valuation methods and calculations at a breakneck pace, it introduced mistakes that were difficult to catch. But the junior analysts developed a deeper knowledge of the multiple companies and other stakeholders involved in an M&A and of the relevant industry and learned how to manage the entire valuation process. Rather than function as a cog in a system they didn't understand, they engaged in work that positioned them to take on more-senior roles. Another benefit was the discovery that, far from being interchangeable, the software packages they'd been using to create inputs for analysis sometimes produced valuations of a given company that were billions of dollars apart. Had the analysts remained siloed, that might never have come to light.

Tapping frontline know-how

As discussed, robotic surgeons are isolated from the patient and so lack a holistic sense of the work, making it harder for residents to gain the skills they need. To understand the bigger picture, residents sometimes turn to scrub techs, who see the procedure in its totality: the patient's entire body; the position and movement of the robot's arms; the activities of the anesthesiologist, the nurse, and others around the patient; and all the instruments and supplies from start to finish. The best scrubs have paid careful attention during thousands of procedures. When residents shift from the console to the bedside, therefore, some bypass the attending and go straight to these "superscrubs" with technical questions, such as whether the intra-abdominal pressure is unusual, or when to clear the field of fluid or of smoke from cauterization. They do this despite norms and often unbeknownst to the attending.

And what about the start-up managers who were outsourcing jobs to workers in the Philippines and Las Vegas? They were expected to remain laser focused on raising capital and hiring engineers. But a few spent time with the frontline contract workers to learn how and why they made the matches they did. This led to insights that helped the company refine its processes for acquiring and cleaning data—an essential step in creating a stable platform. Similarly, some attentive managers spent time with the customer service reps in Las Vegas as they helped workers contend with the system. These "ride alongs" led the managers to divert some resources to improving the user interface, helping to sustain the start-up as it continued to acquire new users and recruit engineers who could build the robust machine learning systems it needed to succeed.

Redesigning roles

The new work methods we create to deploy intelligent machines are driving a variety of shadow learning tactics that restructure work or alter how performance is measured and rewarded. A surgical resident may decide early on that she isn't going to do robotic surgery as a senior physician and will therefore consciously minimize her robotic rotation. Some nurses I studied prefer the technical troubleshooting involved in robotic assignments, so they surreptitiously avoid open surgical work. Nurses who staff surgical procedures notice emerging preferences and skills and work around blanket staffing policies to accommodate them. People tacitly recognize and develop new roles that are better aligned with the work—whether or not the organization formally does so.

Consider how some police chiefs reframed expectations for beat cops who were having trouble integrating predictive analytics into their work. Brayne found that many officers assigned to patrol PredPol's "boxes" appeared to be less productive on traditional measures such as number of arrests, citations, and FIs (field interview cards—records made by officers of their contacts with citizens, typically people who seem suspicious). FIs are particularly important in AI-assisted policing, because they provide crucial input data for predictive systems even when no arrests result. When cops went where the system directed them, they often made no arrests, wrote no tickets, and created no FIs. Recognizing that these traditional measures discouraged beat cops from following PredPol's recommendations, a few chiefs sidestepped standard practice and publicly and privately praised officers not for making arrests and delivering citations but for learning to work with the algorithmic assignments. As one captain said, "Good, fine, but we are telling you where the probability of a crime is at, so sit there, and if you come in with a zero [no crimes], that is a success." These chiefs were taking a risk by encouraging what many saw as bad policing, but in doing so they were helping to move the law enforcement culture toward a future in which the police will increasingly collaborate with intelligent machines, whether or not PredPol remains in the tool kit.

Curating solutions

Trainees in robotic surgery occasionally took time away from their formal responsibilities to create, annotate, and share play-by-play recordings of expert procedures. In addition to providing a resource for themselves and others, making the recordings helped them learn, because they had to classify phases of the work, techniques, types of failures, and responses to surprises.

Faculty members who were struggling to build online courses while maintaining their old-school skills used similar techniques to master the new technology. EdX provided tools, templates, and training materials to make things easier for instructors, but that wasn't enough. Especially in the beginning, far-flung instructors in resource-strapped institutions took time to experiment with the platform, make notes and videos on their failures and successes, and share them informally with one another online. Establishing these connections was hard, especially when the instructors' institutions were ambivalent about putting content and pedagogy online in the first place.

Shadow learning of a different type occurred among the original users of edX—well-funded, well-supported professors at topflight institutions who had provided early input during the development of the platform. To get the support and resources they needed from edX, they surreptitiously shared techniques for pitching desired changes in the platform, securing funding and staff support, and so on.

Learning from Shadow Learners

Obviously shadow learning is not the ideal solution to the problems it addresses. No one should have to risk getting fired just to master a job. But these practices are hard-won, tested paths in a world where acquiring expertise is becoming more difficult and more important.

The four classes of behavior shadow learners exhibit—seeking struggle, tapping frontline know-how, redesigning roles, and curating solutions—suggest corresponding tactical responses. To take advantage of the lessons shadow learners offer, technologists, managers, experts, and workers themselves should:

- Ensure that learners get opportunities to struggle near the edge of their capacity in real (not simulated) work so that they can make and recover from mistakes

- Foster clear channels through which the best frontline workers can serve as instructors and coaches

- Restructure roles and incentives to help learners master new ways of working with intelligent
  machines

- Build searchable, annotated, crowdsourced "skill
  repositories" containing tools and expert guidance
  that learners can tap and contribute to as needed

The specific approach to these activities depends on
organizational structure, culture, resources, technological
options, existing skills, and, of course, the nature of the
work itself. No single best practice will apply in all circumstances. But a large body of managerial literature explores
each of these, and outside consulting is readily available.

More broadly, my research, and that of my colleagues,
suggests three organizational strategies that may help leverage shadow learning's lessons:

1. Keep studying it

Shadow learning is evolving rapidly as intelligent technologies become more capable. New forms will emerge
over time, offering new lessons. A cautious approach is
critical. Shadow learners often realize that their practices
are deviant and that they could be penalized for pursu-
ing them. (Imagine if a surgical resident made it known

that he sought out the least-skilled attendings to work with.) And middle managers often turn a blind eye to these practices because of the results they produce—as long as the shadow learning isn't openly acknowledged. Thus learners and their managers may be less than forthcoming when an observer, particularly a senior manager, declares that he wants to study how employees are breaking the rules to build skills. A good solution is to bring in a neutral third party who can ensure strict anonymity while comparing practices across diverse cases. My informants came to know and trust me, and they were aware that I was observing work in numerous work groups and facilities, so they felt confident that their identities would be protected. That proved essential in getting them to open up.

2. Adapt the shadow learning practices you find to design organizations, work, and technology

Organizations have often handled intelligent machines in ways that make it easier for a single expert to take more control of the work, reducing dependence on trainees' help. Robotic surgical systems allow senior surgeons to operate with less assistance, so they do. Investment banking systems allow senior partners to exclude junior analysts from complex valuations, so they do. All stakeholders should insist on organizational, technological, and work designs that improve productivity and enhance on-the-job learning. In the LAPD, for example, this would mean moving beyond changing incentives for beat cops to efforts such as redesigning the PredPol user interface, creating new roles to bridge police officers and software engineers, and establishing a cop-curated repository for annotated best practice use cases.

3. Make intelligent machines part of the solution

AI can be built to coach learners as they struggle, coach experts on their mentorship, and connect those two groups in smart ways. For example, when Juho Kim was a doctoral student at MIT, he built ToolScape and LectureScape, which allow for crowdsourced annotation of instructional videos and provide clarification and opportunities for practice where many prior users have paused to look for them. He called this *learnersourcing*. On the hardware side, augmented reality systems are beginning to bring expert instruction and annotation right into the flow of work. Existing applications use tablets or smart glasses to overlay instructions on work in real time. More-sophisticated intelligent systems are expected soon. Such systems might, for example, superimpose a recording of the best welder in the factory on an apprentice welder's visual field to show how the job is done, record the apprentice's attempt to match it, and connect the apprentice to the welder as needed. The growing community of engineers in these domains have mostly been focused on formal training, and the deeper crisis is in on-the-job learning. We need to redirect our efforts there.

Conclusion

For thousands of years, advances in technology have driven the redesign of work processes, and apprentices have learned necessary new skills from mentors. But as we've seen, intelligent machines now motivate us to peel apprentices away from masters, and masters from the work itself, all in the name of productivity. Organizations often unwittingly choose productivity over considered human involvement, and learning on the job is getting harder as a result. Shadow learners are nevertheless finding risky, rule-breaking ways to learn. Organizations that hope to compete in a world filling with increasingly intelligent machines should pay close attention to these "deviants." Their actions provide insight into how the best work will be done in the future, when experts, apprentices, and intelligent machines work, and learn, together.

On-the-job learning has long depended on mentorship, with experts coaching apprentices. But this model is under threat from the headlong introduction of sophisticated analytics, AI, and robotics into many aspects of work. These technologies are moving trainees away from learning opportunities and experts away from the action.

✓ Learners in various fields are figuring out "deviant," rule-breaking work-arounds—"shadow learning"—to overcome these obstacles.

✓ Companies can benefit from studying shadow learners in fields as diverse as surgery, law enforcement, and M&A analysis; their actions provide insight into how the best work will be done in the future, when experts, apprentices, and intelligent machines work, and learn, together.

Adapted from "Learning to Work with Intelligent Machines" in Harvard Business Review, *September–October 2019 (product #R1905K).*

Section 3

THE NEXT TECH TRENDS IN BUSINESS

6

5G'S POTENTIAL, AND WHY BUSINESSES SHOULD START PREPARING FOR IT

by Omar Abbosh and Larry Downes

A new Accenture survey of nearly two thousand technology and business executives in 10 countries revealed deep uncertainty about next-generation mobile network technology, known as 5G.[1] Few of those surveyed, for example, believe industry predictions about the dramatically improved speeds of 5G networks. And more than half don't expect the technology will enable them to do much that they can't already do. Nearly three-quarters said they need help imagining 5G use cases.

These findings suggest that many business leaders understand neither the technology nor its disruptive potential. When fully implemented, 5G is poised to be a very big deal, a far bigger transformation in mobile technology than any previous generational shift. Its speed, capacity, and dramatically reduced power consumption and communications response times, or *latency*, will make possible an astonishing range of innovative new products and services. The economic and social benefits could be enormous.

5G networks rely on much smaller, but more densely deployed, antennae, most attached not to giant cell towers but to existing buildings, light poles, and other physical infrastructure. By packing or *densifying* the network, signals will be carried faster and more reliably, with bandwidth measured not in megabits but rather in *gigabits* per second. Early tests suggest that 5G networks will be as much as one hundred times faster than today's mobile technology.

Part of the disconnect in company leaders' perceptions is no doubt the result of early marketing, with some carriers already offering 5G products before the full technical specification has yet to be completed. Wall Street and others have expressed skepticism, unsure of where the true value of 5G will come from, and who will profit from it (more on that in a moment).

In fact, these remarkable technical features will allow next-generation networks to compete head-on with wired broadband systems, including those built with today's fastest fiber-optic technology.

More to the point, 5G's revolutionary technology will also make possible the kind of disruptive applications that usually leave both investors and users salivating. So why the gap between 5G's possibilities and the lack of urgency and understanding among the executives in our survey?

The answer, we think, is that much of 5G's biggest impact will be diffused across a range of industries and user communities, making its future value both difficult to see and hard to measure.

Our book, *Pivot to the Future*, finds that similar mismatches between the potential of new technologies and their actual, realized benefits are growing, including with artificial intelligence and quantum computing. Most senior executives we surveyed are looking at these technologies through the lens of incremental improvements to today's business, rather than imagining how they could be used to reshape industries and, even more broadly, how they could be applied in the search for solutions to broader social problems, including the environment, poverty, and health care.

This is largely due to the limitations of conventional business thinking. When new innovations disrupt multiple industries or make possible applications that serve new groups of customers (including those who may be unserved or underserved today), traditional approaches to strategy and planning underestimate their real impact, leading to delayed investment and missed opportunities.

These failures accumulate in the form of unrealized gains for enterprises, industries, consumers, and society as a whole—what we call *trapped value*.

To take just one example, 5G networks will supercharge the nascent Internet of Things (IoT), where everyday devices become connected, sending and receiving data to highly local networks and from there in secured form throughout the cloud, including to service providers and device manufacturers.

Where today's IoT offerings, including connected doorbells and thermostats, are often simple and sometimes even gimmicky, a fully connected residence will generate tremendous benefit, especially to aging baby boomers who hope to stay in their homes as long as possible.

With sensors that monitor, and devices that assist, everything from mobility to medication, seniors will be able to age in place at much higher rates, and for longer. Connected robots, 3-D-printed prosthetics, and telehealth services, likewise, will all play a part in the house of the future. To work together, truly smart homes will need 5G's capacity, reliability, energy efficiency, and low latency. (We'll also need better answers to a growing list of questions about user data collection and use.)

That kind of use case could release tremendous trapped value we'll all share, including the potential for reduced health-care costs, improved quality of life, and more diverse and inclusive communities. But because the industries affected and the users benefiting most from these applications are so diffused, few businesses today, including the network operators themselves, can see the value gap that is growing larger every day.

To take a second example, consider the profound impact of smart vehicles, connected roads, and other infrastructure. A 2017 study by Accenture Strategy estimated that smart city applications made possible by 5G networks could create three million new jobs and contribute $500 billion to U.S. GDP over the next seven years, releasing value trapped in the form of productivity lost today to time wasted in traffic and reduced pollution from vehicles traveling more efficiently in "platoons."[2]

Those kinds of benefits, though large, are difficult to calculate in a typical strategy exercise. Even more challenging to factor in is one of the greatest hopes for smart transportation: a dramatic reduction in vehicle fatalities. In the United States alone, just a 10% decline in roadway deaths would translate to four thousand lives saved *every year*. While we have a way to go before autonomous driving technology is available at such a scale, that kind of positive change would impact everything from insurance to vehicle design, releasing trapped value that would be difficult to overestimate.

Beyond smart homes and cities, the speed, capacity, and reliability of 5G networks will accelerate new innovations in equally impressive ways elsewhere. Agriculture, for example, could become substantially more efficient from connected sensors in the ground, drones patrolling crops, and integrated weather tracking technology. Mobile entertainment also stands to be enhanced by 5G's speed, and in particular its reduced latency, to offer ever-higher-quality video, supplemented with new types of interactions from augmented and virtual reality.

There's no shortage of predictions about the potential for 5G networks. But like many new technologies, and as our survey makes clear, there's also a great deal of uncertainty about the when, how, where, and who. Full 5G deployment may be five years away—maybe more depending on how regulators and local governments respond to both the opportunities and challenges. The applications we've identified may come sooner or later, along with the many that haven't even been thought of yet.

Still, if incumbent businesses don't pick up the pace in preparing for 5G, the resulting gaps will inevitably attract new entrants and startups, unleashing the kind of sudden disruptions that have unsettled mature industries including entertainment (iTunes and Netflix), transportation (Uber and Lyft), and manufacturing (3-D printing), to name a few.

That's why we recommend an aggressive but measured approach to planning for and investing in 5G today. It makes little sense for companies in affected industries (increasingly, all of them) to bet on one particular technology or application. But at the same time, the old approach of waiting for new 5G-powered markets to emerge and jumping in later as a so-called fast follower won't work either.

That's because even when disruptors are slow to gain traction, once they do, the race to profit is often over as soon as it starts. If you weren't already warmed up and on the starting line, your chances of winning will be virtually zero.

What's more, many of the new applications 5G technology makes possible will be nurtured by interconnected ecosystems that cross traditional supply-chain and industry borders. Any hope of capturing even a fraction of the value 5G will ultimately release will require early and sustained intervention, perhaps in the form of industry consortia, along with a balanced portfolio of corporate venture funding. The time is now to begin identifying partners and experimenting with new forms of collaboration and co-investment.

You need to keep improving on today's business while keeping a closer watch on how 5G markets emerge. That's the only way to be ready to scale rapidly with new offerings as the unknowns dissolve over time.

TAKEAWAYS

Next-generation mobile network technology, known as 5G, has enormous disruptive potential. When fully implemented, it will bring a far bigger transformation in mobile technology than any previous generational shift.

✓ 5G's speed, capacity, and dramatically reduced power consumption and latency could make an astonishing range of innovative new products and services possible, from truly smart homes and cities to autonomous cars that travel in "platoons" to reduce traffic.

✓ If incumbent businesses don't pick up the pace in preparing for 5G, the resulting gaps will inevitably attract new entrants and startups, unleashing the kind of sudden disruptions that have unsettled mature industries in the past.

✓ Many of the new 5G applications will be nurtured by interconnected ecosystems, perhaps in the form of industry consortia, along with a balanced portfolio of corporate venture funding. The time is now to begin identifying partners as 5G markets are emerging.

NOTES

1. "Business and Technology Executives Underestimate the Disruptive Prospects of 5G Technology, Accenture Study Finds," Accenture.com, February 25, 2019, https://newsroom.accenture .com/news/business-and-technology-executives-underestimate -the-disruptive-prospects-of-5g-technology-accenture-study-finds .htm.

2. "How 5G Can Help Municipalities Become Vibrant Smart Cities," Accenture.com, 2017, https://newsroom.accenture.com /content/1101/files/Accenture_5G-Municipalities-Become-Smart -Cities.pdf.

Adapted from "5G's Potential, and Why Businesses Should Start Preparing for It," on hbr.org, March 5, 2019 (product #H04TUD).

CAN BIOMETRICS PREDICT A VIRAL MARKETING CAMPAIGN?

by Jacob L. H. Jones, Matthew Gillespie, and Kelsey Libert

T he difference between content that goes viral and content that fails to find an audience depends on a single, critical moment: a person seeing the share button and deciding whether or not to click.

Unlocking how to predict what will happen at this moment would be akin to discovering the holy grail of marketing research. Simply asking people what kind of content they would share doesn't do a great job of anticipating actual outcomes. However, researchers can utilize physiological markers to measure emotional responses to content—which exist not just in the mind but also in the body—to better understand what makes someone click "share."

In a recent study, people were shown a mix of popular and unpopular content. We asked participants the usual follow-up questions, such as: "Were you engaged in this content? Do you think you would share this?" and so on. By recording an electrophysiological signal called galvanic skin response (GSR)—a response that is constantly changing in an individual, though rarely noticed—during the study, we were able to predict the viral outcome of a piece of content significantly better than was possible via any of the usual survey measures.

Can We Anticipate Viral Content Before It Goes Live?

What we know for certain is that *people* are at the heart of viral outcomes (unless you are leveraging bots or other automated methods to drive traffic, in which case, we can't help you). From previous marketing research, we know that the emotions evoked in readers are critical to the likelihood a piece of content will go viral and that people are more likely to share content that is highly arousing. These findings are important, but how can you test whether content is likely to go viral without subjecting it to the scrutiny of the internet?

Typically, predictions around how content will perform are formulated using a combination of content topic analysis and self-report of measures such as "likelihood to share." We decided to extend these metrics to include a known physiological measure, GSR, to see whether there was predictive value in how the body itself responded to pieces of our own agency's content that had highly variable success in the field.

Why GSR? Electrophysiology measures have been around for a long time, but the technical and economic barriers to using them in marketing research were fairly high until recently. The average marketer was skeptical of their utility, particularly since these costly types of methods had not been definitively shown to produce a clear advantage over cheaper, more accessible behavioral methods. Over time, prices have decreased, and though these devices still require a strong technical understanding, they are not as difficult to use as they once were. Galvanic skin response, which measures the skin's resistance to a very mild electrical current, has been demonstrated to be a strong predictor of emotional arousal, and emotional arousal is known to be a crucial ingredient for viral content.[1]

Getting people to self-report their emotional arousal has long been an attractive option for researchers: These surveys are cheap and make it easy to collect data from a large group of people. However, there are several limitations to self-reported data. Telescoping, selective memory, and the availability heuristic are just three of the dozens of ways certain participants can obscure the results of your study. Not to mention the "bot crisis"—large-scale corruption of data validity from participants either not paying attention as they complete surveys or leveraging bots to auto-complete surveys with fake data—which has plagued the online platforms that marketers and academics utilize to recruit participants.

In general, people are just pretty bad at knowing how they feel and why they feel that way. Just look into the misattribution effect for proof. People constantly misinterpret their physiological state to the emotional context they find themselves in. This effect explains why you may think a fear response is actually sexual attraction or why a rainy day might make your bad mood worse. It is also why drinking coffee or watching horror movies makes great dates.

In our study, we examined content from 15 highly successful Fractl content marketing campaigns (average social shares = 21,358.07) and 15 of our low-performing campaigns (average social shares = 11.07). We compiled the graphics most prominently featured in the publisher coverage earned by each campaign and showed them to 22 participants. We used only most prominently featured assets for two reasons. First, this allowed us to include a wider variety of stimuli in the study; if we used entire projects with several images each, the number of campaigns sampled would need to be much smaller. Second, because of where these graphics were placed, they were the ones most likely to be viewed and shared by readers.

Prior to coming into the lab, participants were given a qualifying/demographic survey. Additionally, we collected self-reported interest in all the content verticals we explored (this included items like *sports data*, *political data*, *health and wellness data*, *workplace data*, etc.). We used a Shimmer GSR unit to gather galvanic skin response data.

After viewing each image, participants filled out a brief survey where they reported their levels of interest, enjoyment, surprise, and understanding of the content. We also asked how likely participants were to share each image and how engaging they found each image overall. Participants rated almost every qualifier on a 5-point Likert—a scale with an odd number of answer anchors that allow researchers to assess the attitudes of participants (for example, a five-star rating system for businesses). The question regarding how engaging the content was to them was rated on a dichotomous 9-point scale—a scale that ranges from one adjective to its polar opposite (for example, *1 for extremely boring to 9 for extremely engaging*).

Our hypotheses were as follows:

1. The content in the highly viral group will elicit more emotional arousal in our participants, leading to greater electrodermal activity.

2. Participants' electrodermal activity would be more predictive of viral outcomes if the participant had previously expressed interest in that content vertical.

3. The behavioral survey methods will be less predictive of viral outcomes than the biometrics.

What we found was: There was a significant difference between the high and low viral content for phasic galvanic skin response (phasic GSR refers to the portion of the data that corresponds directly to a participant's response to a stimulus).

This effect was not reduced by whether or not participants reported being interested in a given piece of content: both "low interest" and "high interest" items showed the same pattern of galvanic skin response. There was no significant difference in the predictive ability of participants' galvanic skin response if they were interested in the content vertical or not.

In plain English, this means that whether or not someone actually told us they were interested in a type of content, their body's response still predicted how that piece of content eventually performed on the internet (see figure 7-1).

We also found that participants' self-reported data—typically a cornerstone of marketing research—was not able to predict which content was eventually successful. There was no significant difference between the high-viral and low-viral content in terms of how participants rated their understanding, how likely they would be to share it, how surprising they found it, how much they enjoyed it, and how engaging they found it.

Can Virality Be Predicted?

The more viral a campaign was, the greater galvanic skin response our participants had while viewing it. This held

FIGURE 7-1

Skin response to viral content categorized by participants' self-reported interest

Galvanic skin response is a technique that measures emotional arousal based on the skin's resistance to electricity. It was able to predict which content eventually went viral regardless of whether or not study participants found the topic interesting.

Normalized mean response in microsiemens

High-interest content

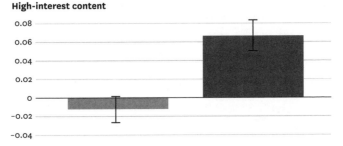

Low-interest content

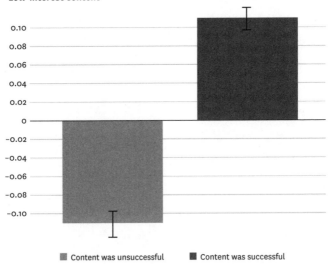

■ Content was unsuccessful   ■ Content was successful

Note: Microsiemens are a unit measuring electrical conductance.
Source: Fractl

true regardless of self-reported interest in the campaign vertical; in fact, all our self-reported metrics were much less useful than galvanic skin response. Factors such as how well our participants understood the content, how much they enjoyed it, how surprised they were by it, how likely they were to share it personally, or how engaging they found it did not correlate with how likely the content was to go viral.

The intersection of electrophysiology measures and marketing is a new and exciting field. Introducing biometrics such as galvanic skin response, eye tracking, and EEG (electroencephalogram) to a market research repertoire may yield insights previously unattainable to marketers. Though we still cannot perfectly predict what makes content go viral online, neurometrics help us get a clearer view into the minds of digital content consumers.

TAKEAWAYS

What separates an article that goes viral from the rest depends on a single moment: a person deciding whether or not to click the share button. Being able to predict what will happen would be akin to discovering the holy grail of marketing research.

- ✓ According to research, self-reported factors such as how well participants understood the content, how much they enjoyed it, how surprised they were by it, how likely they were to share it personally, or how engaging they found it did not correlate with how likely the content was to go viral.

- ✓ Physiological markers, however, can be used to measure emotional responses to content. By recording an electrophysiological signal called galvanic skin response (GSR), researchers were able to predict the viral outcome of a piece of content significantly better.

- ✓ Introducing biometrics such as GSR, eye tracking, and EEG (electroencephalogram) to a market research repertoire may yield insights previously unattainable to marketers.

NOTE

1. Dominik R. Bach, Karl J. Friston, and Raymond J. Dolan, "Analytic Measures for Quantification of Arousal from Spontaneous Skin Conductance Fluctuations," *International Journal of Psycho-*

physiology 76, no. 1 (April 2010): 52–55, https://www.ncbi.nlm.nih .gov/pmc/articles/PMC2877802/; Kerry Jones, Kelsey Libert, and Kristin Tynski, "The Emotional Combinations That Make Stories Go Viral," hbr.org, May 23, 2016, https://hbr.org/2016/05/research -the-link-between-feeling-in-control-and-viral-content.

Adapted from "Can Biometrics Predict a Viral Marketing Campaign?" on hbr.org, January 10, 2019 (product #H04OYU).

8

HOW WEARABLE AI WILL AMPLIFY HUMAN INTELLIGENCE

by Lauren Golembiewski

Imagine that your team is meeting to decide whether to continue an expensive marketing campaign. After a few minutes, it becomes clear that nobody has the metrics on-hand to make the decision. You chime in with a solution and ask Amazon's virtual assistant Alexa to back you up with information: "Alexa, how many users did we convert to customers last month with Campaign A?" And Alexa responds with the answer. You just amplified your team's intelligence with AI. But this is just the tip of the iceberg.

Intelligence amplification is the use of technology to augment human intelligence. And a paradigm shift is on the horizon, where new devices will offer less intrusive, more intuitive ways to amplify our intelligence.

Hearables, or wireless in-ear computational earpieces, are an example of intelligence-amplification devices that have been adopted recently and rapidly. An example is Apple's AirPods, which are smart earbuds that connect to Apple devices and integrate with Siri via voice commands. Apple has also filed a patent for earbuds equipped with biometric sensors that could record data such as a user's temperature, heart rate, and movement. Similarly, Google's Pixel Buds give users direct access to the Google Assistant and its powerful knowledge graph. Google Assistant seamlessly connects users to information stored in Google platforms, like email and calendar management. Google Assistant also provides users with highly personalized recommendations, helps automate personal communication, and off-loads monotonous tasks like setting timers, managing lists, and controlling IoT devices.

While technology on the market today affords humans a multitude of capabilities unavailable to them even just a decade ago, there is still an opportunity for improvement and refinement. The power and prevalence of smartphones allows humans to easily amplify intelligence, but the use of these devices is often obtrusive. It's all too common to see people in public completely absorbed with the little screens in their hands rather than their surroundings, or to have social situations interrupted by someone pulling out their smartphone to check a notification or complete a search. Hearables, along with other voice-enabled devices, allow users to seek information and complete tasks without a screen interface, but they are inherently less discreet than smartphones. Users must speak their questions and commands aloud, which may not be desirable or possible in certain situations. This lack of discretion diminishes the impact of the voice-enabled intelligence-amplifying interfaces as it limits the contexts in which they can be used.

The need for an intelligence-amplifying device that is less obtrusive than a smartphone and more discreet than a voice interface is clear. Many technologists and entrepreneurs are working to create the next revolutionary intelligence-amplifying device that will solve the problems of its predecessors while giving users seamless access to advanced AI systems.

The Next Generation of Intelligence Amplification

We're quickly moving toward a world where AI will more seamlessly help to power our human intelligence and interactions.

Consider AlterEgo, a project originating from the MIT Media Lab—an intelligence-amplification device that uses *silent* speech recognition, also known as internal articulation, to measure the electrical signals the brain sends to the internal speech organs. AlterEgo is a non-invasive device that's worn over the ear and along the jawline. The signals it measures are part of the voluntary nervous system, meaning users must intentionally *think* of speaking words to trigger the device—a feature that sets it apart from other brain-computer interfaces (BCI) that are capable of receiving signals directly from the brain. The AlterEgo device translates these silent user signals into commands to control other systems, such as IoT devices, and query information, say from a Google search. Users control the device without opening their mouths and without any externally observable movements. They simply have to *think* about the words they would have asked Siri or a smart speaker out loud. Information is then relayed back to the user through audio. (AlterEgo uses bone-conduction audio to respond back to users, which completes the discreet information loop silently.) The entire interaction is completely internal to the user—almost like speaking to oneself. AlterEgo's creators hope that this silent information loop will make people's interactions with the technology both unobtrusive and discreet.

Arnav Kapur, a PhD student at MIT who leads the AlterEgo project, described their vision in a recent interview: "Speaking is not private, but you are in total control of it. Thinking is completely private, but sometimes you're not in control of all your thoughts. We're trying to make something that's right in between those two ends of the spectrum, but that brings the best of both worlds."

It's clear that Kapur and the rest of the AlterEgo team are driven to give users a positive experience by balancing the AI's intimate access to the user with discretion, and the user's ultimate control of their sensitive data. Kapur adds, "We thought a lot about what the ethical issues are with this technology being used in the wild; the user is in control of the technology at all times, and the technology is not intrusive. Privacy is not an afterthought."

Augmented reality devices represent another interesting foray into modern intelligence amplification. Google Glass, smart eyewear that failed in the consumer market, is now being used in enterprise and industrial applications. For example, employers such as GE are implementing smart eyewear technology to increase the efficiency of their warehouse and manufacturing workers. Technicians at GE are able to use guided instructions overlaid on their field of view to increase their productivity and reduce errors while servicing or repairing manufacturing equipment.

There is also an opportunity to leverage the user data that these new devices capture to create highly personalized experiences. Pattie Maes, MIT professor and advisor to AlterEgo, says, "Systems that have an awareness of the user—their [mental and emotional] state, their intentions—will ultimately be less intrusive and more useful, because they can customize the information that is being provided to the situation at hand." Much of the industry is already thinking about how the insights extrapolated by AI will be used by the companies building intelligence-amplifying devices. Futurist Amy Webb warns of large companies like Amazon being able to wield deeper influence over their customers, such as selling medicine to customers they believe are ill or depressed.[1]

Preparing for the Next Era of Personal Computing

There is an immense opportunity for business leaders to capitalize on intelligence-amplifying technology. Each new device further reduces the barriers between an individual's and an organization's knowledge and provides a new platform on which businesses can build applications to connect with customers, employees, and partners. Intelligence-amplifying devices will be the primary means by which individuals interact with the world, so business leaders and stakeholders should plan for how their organizations will embrace the coming changes in personal computing.

Designing and developing experiences for intelligence-amplifying devices will require new technical skills and more collaboration across disciplines. Data scientists, researchers, designers, and engineers will all need to understand the technology powering intelligence-amplifying devices in order to create innovative and useful applications that appropriately leverage AI.

As consumers and employees integrate more of their lives into the digital space with new intelligence-amplifying devices, organizations must consider and address issues of data transparency, privacy, and autonomy. These themes are already at the forefront of user awareness and concern in the wake of the many high-profile data breaches over the past few years. Consumers are rightfully wary of handing over their data to big businesses who may use it to manipulate consumers or sell it to other businesses with that intention. As more personal data is captured with these devices, and as AI is able to extrapolate more details about consumers, everyone is more vulnerable. Businesses should focus on building trust with consumers by being transparent with their data practices and prioritizing privacy and autonomy when developing and implementing more personalized, intelligence-amplifying technologies.

Many businesses are already augmenting their workforce with AI in the areas of communication, sales, support, and decision making. Some experts believe that intelligence amplification could be an antidote to automation-related job loss by making augmented humans indispensable. Because intelligence amplification builds upon existing human intelligence and all that it encompasses, it can be seen as more powerful than AI alone. It's time for business leaders and stakeholders to consider how to successfully embrace this new era of personal computing.

TAKEAWAYS

AI-enabled wearables are offering less intrusive, more intuitive ways to power human intelligence and interactions. Each new device further reduces knowledge barriers and provides a new platform on which businesses can build applications to connect with customers, employees, and partners.

- ✓ Intelligence-amplifying devices will become the primary means by which individuals interact with the world. Business leaders and stakeholders should plan now for how their organizations will embrace the coming changes in personal computing.

- ✓ Data scientists, researchers, designers, and engineers will all need to understand the technology powering intelligence-amplifying devices in order to create innovative and useful applications that appropriately leverage AI.

- ✓ As more personal data is captured by wearables, and as AI is able to extrapolate more details about consumers, everyone is more vulnerable to privacy abuses. Businesses should focus on building trust with consumers by being transparent with their data practices and prioritizing privacy and autonomy.

NOTE

1. Katherine Schwab, "Amazon Could Soon Force You to Go on a Diet," fastcompany.com, March 21, 2019, https://www.fastcompany

.com/90322180/amazon-could-soon-force-you-to-go-on-a-diet
-according-to-one-futurist; Jon Brodkin, "Amazon Patents
Alexa Tech to Tell If You're Sick, Depressed and Sell You Meds,"
arstechnica.com, October 11, 2018, https://arstechnica.com
/gadgets/2018/10/amazon-patents-alexa-tech-to-tell-if-youre-sick
-depressed-and-sell-you-meds/.

*Adapted from "How Wearable AI Will Amplify Human Intelligence," on hbr.org,
April 30, 2019 (product #H04XG5).*

9

THE ERA OF ANTISOCIAL SOCIAL MEDIA

by Sara Wilson

S ocial platforms are still reporting robust growth—
yes, even Facebook—despite a growing chorus of
opposition. Social conversation continues to shape
everything from culture to the media cycle to our most
intimate relationships. And we now spend more time
than ever on our phones, with endless scrolling through
our social feeds being a chief reason why.

But dig a little deeper, and a more nuanced picture
emerges about social media users today that has important

implications for the ways in which brands reach customers. Specifically, when you look at who is—and more importantly, who is *not*—driving the growth and popularity of social platforms, a key demographic appears to be somewhat in retreat: young people.

For example, 2019 findings from Edison Research and Triton Digital show social media usage overall among Americans 12 to 34 years old across several platforms has either leveled off or is waning, while 2019 research from GlobalWebIndex suggests that the amount of time millennial and Gen Z audiences spend on many social platforms is either flat, declining, or not rising as greatly as it has in years past.[1]

To understand what's driving this shift, you need only talk to young people. They're saying that after years spent constructing carefully curated online identities and accumulating heaps of online "friends," they want to be themselves and make real friends based on shared interests. They're also craving privacy, safety, and a respite from the throngs of people on social platforms—throngs that now usually include their parents.

To reach these younger audiences on social media, marketers are going to have to rethink their approach. The first step is to understand the distinct characteristics of these more closed, and often more private and interactive, online spaces. Since I believe that naming a trend helps provide a framework for understanding it, I have dubbed these spaces *digital campfires.*

If social media can feel like a crowded airport terminal where everyone is allowed but no one feels particularly excited to be there, digital campfires offer a more intimate oasis where smaller groups of people are excited to gather around shared interests.

I've identified three categories of digital campfires: private messaging, micro-communities, and shared experiences. Some digital campfires are a combination of all three.

Let's examine the characteristics of each, as well as how brands are successfully navigating the challenges of reaching the audiences in these environments.

Private-Messaging Campfires

Private or small-group messaging—usually but not always with one's real-life friends—is the primary purpose for gathering.

In a 2019 survey from ZAK, a youth-focused creative agency, nearly two-thirds of the 1,000 people polled, all under 30, said they prefer to talk in private message threads rather than on open forums and feeds.[2] Sixty percent of respondents stated that talking in private groups means they can "share more openly."

Private-messaging campfires often exist on traditional social platforms. Facebook Messenger and WhatsApp are among the most well-known examples. According to the ZAK survey, 38% of people under 30 *only* use Facebook for the private messenger function. Instagram, the rare platform showing an upward usage trend among younger Americans, recently launched a new standalone app, called Threads, designed expressly for quick-fire messaging with close friends via the camera and text.

For the most part, brands aren't invited into these private chats. Some have responded by adapting similar technologies, like texting (whether with actual humans or human-seeming chatbots), to mimic the intimacy of personal conversations with friends.

For example, there's Text Rex, a members-only, text message–based, personalized restaurant recommendation service from the dining review site The Infatuation (a favorite among millennial foodies). Users can text questions like "Where should I take my date in Midtown Manhattan?" or "What's the best midday sushi in Santa Monica?" and receive answers from actual humans (Infatuation staffers).

Similarly, there's Community—another text-based service that launched last year to help corporations, stars, and high-profile individuals facilitate direct conversations with their fans via text messaging "without getting buried by social feeds and algorithms." Community's primary users are celebrities (among them: Kerry Washington, Amy Schumer, and Paul McCartney). But some fashion and lifestyle brands like Madhappy, APL, and Beautycon have already signed on, and the opportunity for brands to speak more directly to their customers via a channel they're already using is a promising development.

Tip: This is the hardest campfire for marketers to penetrate. Get to know your audience intimately in ways that go way beyond simple demographics. Specifically, work to understand their habits—especially how they consume content and communicate across multiple platforms—and use this to inform the channels on which you communicate with them. Think about how you can reach customers by mimicking their behavior.

Micro-Community Campfires

Primarily interactive private or semiprivate forums where people gather around interests, beliefs, or passions.

Like the private-messaging campfires, micro-community campfires often live on traditional social platforms. Facebook Groups are probably the best-known example. The "close friends" feature within Instagram Stories has become a tool some influencers are using to share exclusive content and interact with small groups of their followers, for a fee. Slack, best known as a workplace messaging tool, is also a place where micro-communities are connecting, often around shared professional interests.

YouTube has long been a hub for hyperspecific communities, and that's still the case today, especially among teens. Sure, anyone can watch or engage with a YouTube video, but the cornucopia of channels means there's something for every conceivable niche interest. For a user, the effect of wading through a vast sea of content to stumble upon something meaningful—combined with the intimacy engendered by the direct-to-camera style of videos on the platform, and the loyalty that comes from subscribing to creator channels—can feel revelatory. (The same cannot be said of the Chinese-owned app TikTok, which, while growing at a phenomenal clip, is largely oriented around the consumption of a seemingly endless feed of entertaining videos served up by an algorithm. It does not allow the user to intentionally connect to specific interest communities.)

Micro-community campfires can also spark in unexpected places. Young people are gathering, for example, on Discord—a voice and text chat platform designed for gamers, which has become something of an under-the-radar hub for beauty obsessives, with multiple servers devoted to topics like advice about makeup or cruelty-free products.

Brands can tap into existing micro-community campfires by partnering with influencers, or they can invest time and resources to build their own campfires from scratch—a heavier lift, of course, but if the brands doing it well are any indication, it's an effort that is well worth it.

One example is Sprite, which spearheaded a campaign for the Latin American market in 2019 called "No Estás Solo" ("You Are Not Alone"). Working with an agency, the company used data from Google to determine personal pain points that young people were searching. It then set up Reddit forums, each helmed by an influencer who had personal experience with issues such as feeling like you're in the wrong body. The outcome: poignant personal discussions about loneliness, all led by Sprite.

Another example is the private Slack group created by beauty brand Glossier, often called one of millennials' most trusted brands. Created exclusively for its best customers to talk about all things beauty, organize meetups, and discuss products, the brand credits the group with helping to co-create one of its now-top-selling products, Milky Jelly Cleanser. At one time, this type of forum might have been dubbed "market research." Today, it also serves as an engine for fandom, while simultaneously allowing the company to be nimble and responsive to anything that is discussed there.

Tip: These campfires are not indexed by Google or advertised on the platforms themselves, so they're hard to find by traditional means. Study your audience to find breadcrumbs that will lead you to their micro-community campfires. Then, partner with an existing campfire or create your own.

Shared-Experience Campfires

Private or public forums where participating in a shared experience—often around a specific shared interest—with a like-minded community is the primary purpose for gathering.

Perhaps the best example of this type of campfire is Fortnite, a multiplayer video game that has more than 200 million users, up to 8 million of whom are online at any given time. The game has been called a de facto social network thanks to the role it occupies in the lives of its players: Indeed, half of teens say they use it to keep up with their friends—some of whom they've never actually met in person—with most spending six to ten hours each week on the platform. In 2019, the EDM artist Marshmello staged a virtual concert inside the game that 10.7 million people "attended." Fortnite is a form of entertainment, but more than that, it's a catalyst for bringing together like-minded people for a shared experience. And the game's steep learning curve lends it an aura of exclusivity.

The live broadcasting and viewing platform Twitch serves a similar function. Live streamers, primarily gamers, broadcast their own gameplay, usually with audio commentary, for fans who can watch and interact via chat. Twitch users consumed 592 billion minutes of livestream content in 2019, and Twitch has recently pushed into nongaming categories like music and sports. As with Fortnite, the primary draw to Twitch is its entertainment value, but the "stickiness" comes from the community and sense of excitement that forms around a shared interest or individual.

So how can marketers zero in on the right shared-experience campfires for their audience? As with the other campfires, they must first identify the communities and parts of the culture that their brand fits into. Then, they must determine the online experiences these audiences seek. Brands like the NFL, Marvel, and Nike have done just that, leveraging Fortnite, for example, to reach their audiences by selling skins (stylized weapons and outfits for players' in-game avatars), creating branded mash-up game modes, and doing limited-edition product drops inside the game.

Tip: Customization is key. Don't simply replicate what you're doing on other platforms—it will come across as ham-fisted. Instead, pay close attention to the behavior of the people in the campfire you want to reach, think about what value you can bring to them, then get creative about the products and messaging you'll use to engage them.

Without question, the digital campfire trend is firmly on the radar of the big social platforms. "Today we already see that private messaging, ephemeral stories, and small groups are by far the fastest growing areas of online communication," Mark Zuckerberg wrote in a March 2019 public post, announcing a strategic shift toward more closed, private modes of communication.[3]

Zuckerberg is paying attention to this shift not only because the data shows that Facebook is losing young audiences but also because redirecting attention to more private modes of communication represents a major challenge for the company.[4] About 98% of Facebook's revenue comes from advertising, and people in smaller, more closed forums are much harder for advertisers to reach at scale.[5]

It is neither simple nor straightforward to reach audiences gathered around digital campfires. But as traditional social platforms grow, they become more crowded, and it becomes more difficult and expensive to reach people there anyway. In light of this, digital campfires become a much more attractive alternative—one that requires more groundwork and more careful tending, but one that could potentially have big payoffs for brands in terms of loyalty, retention, and long-term love.

TAKEAWAYS

Young people are retreating from public social platforms and are gravitating toward more intimate "digital campfires." It can be a challenge for brands to reach these audiences, but as traditional social platforms become more crowded, digital campfires can become an attractive alternative. There are three types, and each requires a different approach to reach participants:

✓ *Private-messaging campfires* are small-group messaging—usually but not always with one's real-life friends. Facebook Messenger and WhatsApp are among the most well-known examples.

✓ *Micro-community campfires* are interactive private or semiprivate forums where people gather around interests, beliefs, or passions. Facebook Groups are an example.

✓ *Shared-experience campfires* are private or public forums where participating in a shared experience with a like-minded community is the purpose for gathering. An example is the multiplayer video game Fortnite.

NOTES

1. Jay Baer, "Social Media Usage Statistics for 2019 Reveal Surprising Shifts," convinceandconvert.com, https://www.convinceandconvert.com/social-media-research/social-media-usage-statistics/; Ashley Viens, "Visualizing Social Media Use by Generation," September 21, 2019, visualcapitalist.com, https://www.visualcapitalist.com/visualizing-social-media-use-by-generation/.

2. "New Research by ZAK on 18–30 Year Olds Demonstrates a Generation Turning Their Backs on the Social Media Giants," lovelymobile.news, July 3, 2019, https://lovelymobile.news/new-research-by-zak-on-18-30-year-olds-demonstrates-a-generation-turning-their-backs-on-the-social-media-giants/.

3. Mark Zuckerberg, "A Privacy-Focused Vision for Social Networking," Facebook post, March 6, 2019, https://www.facebook.com/notes/mark-zuckerberg/a-privacy-focused-vision-for-social-networking/10156700570096634/.

4. Olivia Moore and Justine Moore, "Is Facebook Dead to Gen Z?," techcrunch.com, December 12, 2019, https://techcrunch.com /2019/12/12/is-facebook-dead-to-gen-z/.

5. J. Clement, "Facebook: Advertising Revenue Worldwide 2009–2019," statista.com, February 28, 2020, https://www.statista .com/statistics/271258/facebooks-advertising-revenue-worldwide/.

Adapted from "The Era of Antisocial Social Media," on hbr.org, February 5, 2020 (product #H05E5G).

Section 4

BIG TECH, BIG PROBLEMS

10

WHY IT'S SO HARD FOR USERS TO CONTROL THEIR DATA

by Bhaskar Chakravorti

A recent IBM study found that 81% of consumers say they have become more concerned about how their data is used online.[1] But most users continue to hand over their data online and tick consent boxes impatiently, giving rise to a "privacy paradox" where users' concerns aren't reflected in their behaviors. It's a daunting challenge for regulators and companies alike to navigate the future of data governance.

In my view, we're missing a system that defines and grants users *digital agency*—the ability to own the rights to their personal data, manage access to this data, and potentially be compensated fairly for such access. This would make data similar to other forms of personal property: a home, a bank account, or even a mobile phone number. But before we can imagine such a state, we need to examine three central questions: Why don't users care enough to take actions that match their concerns? What are the possible solutions? Why is this so difficult?

Why Don't Users' Actions Match Their Concerns?

To start, data is intangible. We don't actively hand it over. As a by-product of our online activity, it is easy to ignore or forget about. A lot of data harvesting is invisible to the consumer—they see the results in marketing offers, free services, customized feeds, tailored ads, and beyond.

Second, even if users wanted to negotiate more data agency, they have little leverage. Normally, in well-functioning markets, customers can choose from a range of competing providers. But this is not the case if the service is a widely used digital platform. For many, leaving a platform like Facebook feels like it would come at a high cost in terms of time and effort and that they have no other option for an equivalent service with connections to the same people. Plus, many people use their Facebook log-ins on numerous apps and services. On top of that, Facebook has bought up many of its natural alternatives, like Instagram. It's equally hard to switch from other major platforms, like Google or Amazon, without a lot of personal effort.

Third, while a majority of American users believe more regulation is needed, they are not as enthusiastic about broad regulatory solutions being imposed.[2] Instead, they would prefer to have better data management tools at their disposal. However, managing one's own data would be complex—and that would deter users from embracing such an option.

What Are the Possible Solutions?

One solution is to create mechanisms that give users direct ownership of their data. There are many proposals jostling for attention.

Legislative fixes

Some internet observers believe that the only way to fix the problem is through a comprehensive privacy bill or meaningful, large-scale regulation of Big Tech. Europe's General Data Protection Regulation (GDPR), which is arguably the most comprehensive legislative measure thus far, offers provisions for data portability, giving citizens greater digital agency. However, the European solution has left many dissatisfied with the lack of practicality associated with the rules. As of January 2020, the California Consumer Privacy Act (CCPA) brings a version of GDPR to California residents—and, by extension, residents in other states in many cases, as companies adopt the same standards nationally—who will have the right to know what data of theirs has been collected, delete it, and stop its sale to others, among other things.

The United States also has several other bills under consideration. Senator Mark Warner (D-Va.), Senator Richard Blumenthal (D-Ct.), and Senator Josh Hawley (R-Mo.) have proposed the ACCESS Act that would mandate that social media platforms with over 100 million users in the United States offer users a way to easily move their data to another service. The bill would create conditions for users to retrieve their personal data in a structured and machine-readable format, while the tech companies maintain the necessary interfaces that give access to this data to competing platforms. Hawley and Warner have also coauthored the DASHBOARD Act, which would require data-collecting platforms to be transparent about what data is being collected on users and how it is being monetized.

There is also an "Own Your Own Data Act" in the U.S. Senate, giving a user "an exclusive property right in the data that individual generates on the internet," a cause that has been adopted by former Democratic presidential contender Andrew Yang. Democratic senator Elizabeth Warren has called for an outright breakup of Big Tech, which would increase users' ability to negotiate greater data agency.

Big Tech-led initiatives

The tech companies are attempting to get ahead of the surge of concerns and legislative action and define the ground rules before regulators set them. To be sure, the companies have also been given a prod by the right-to-data-portability requirements under statues like GDPR and CCPA. Facebook has a white paper on data portability, while Google has a facility that allows users to download their data. A challenge remains in that data portability just isn't practical or easy for most users who want a fast way to switch between platforms. To address this, Facebook, Google, Microsoft, Twitter, and Apple have launched a collective initiative, the Data Transfer Project, to move data between platforms without having to download or upload user data; however, progress on the project has been slow.

Ideas from the wider expert and business community

Some of the ideas from the wider business community are conceptual but intuitive because they use recognizable analogies, which makes them worthy of our attention. For example, the musician will.i.am has proposed a concept called *idatity*, combining identity and data as a human right with users being eligible for compensation for transferring it to others. Researchers Eric Posner and Glen Weyl have argued for data to be treated as "labor" and have advocated for mechanisms such as "data labor unions" to collectively bargain with tech companies over payments for access to data. Extending the analogy, they also call for a "minimum data wage" that is equivalent to a standard minimum wage argument but applied to a guaranteed basic compensation to users for producing useful data.

Others, such as the journalist Rana Foroohar, have floated the idea of a public data bank, regulated by elected governments along the lines of the "civic data trust" being considered by Toronto for Google's Sidewalk Labs or data trusts being proposed in general as the concept of a legal trust being applied specifically to the securing of data.

And there are entrepreneurial opportunities. Engineer and World Wide Web inventor, Sir Tim Berners-Lee, launched a startup predicated on the idea of data ownership, where users store their data in a personal data "pod." Users can give or revoke permission to individual apps to read and write to their personal pods.

Indian entrepreneur Nandan Nilekani, a champion of "data democracy," argues that India's technology infrastructure, with his brainchild, the unique ID system Aadhaar, as a foundation, gives India the unique ability to empower every resident with his or her own data. Many Indian banks are taking this forward by preparing to give consumers access to their financial data so that they can directly share it to apply for credit, investment products, or insurance, bypassing the credit ratings agencies as gatekeepers or the lack of credit histories as barriers. This initiative will use third-party mediators and is backed by the country's central bank.

The list goes on. The startup Streamr, which provides infrastructure for users to collectively monetize their data, has an app, Swash, which aims to facilitate a "data union." Yet another venture, Ocean Protocol, intends to facilitate digital agency through a self-managed distributed ledger framework of blockchain.

Despite this multiplicity of ideas, we're no closer to truly meaningful change.

Why Is Data Governance So Hard?

Data, unlike other forms of personal property, is just plain complicated. Any workable solution would need to manage the following 10-point checklist at a minimum:

1. Define what constitutes the personal data to which a user has exclusive rights. For example, a personal photo may contain a picture of a friend tagged by the user. Moving that data could violate the friend's privacy. Alternatively, a user's click-trail tracked by a platform reveals the user's preferences based on the platform's analysis. At what point does that revelation become the platform's intellectual property?

2. Establish criteria to demarcate personal data, anonymized data, and third-party data. To see why this can be difficult, even anonymized data when linked can reveal personally identifiable information; an algorithm was shown to identify 99.98% of Americans by knowing as few as 15 demographic attributes per person.[3] Alternatively, if a user's data links to third-party data deemed harmful or false, can the user remove it

without violating the third party's free-speech rights?

3. Create a transparent—market-based—and universally accepted system of valuing data and compensating users accordingly for trading data. The compensation could be in the form of a tailored service or monetary compensation, while some data may not be tradeable at all.

4. Define standards for how the data is stored, moved, or accessed interoperably across different digital platforms.

5. Establish criteria to evaluate the trade-offs between many needs: interoperability, privacy, cybersecurity. Ease of interoperability, for example, could also reduce cybersecurity.

6. Establish criteria to evaluate the trade-offs between personal data and the use of aggregated data as a "public good"—for training algorithms for societal use, fraud detection, public safety, flagging fake news, etc.

7. Mitigate the transactions costs of negotiating with multiple parties whenever a platform needs

multiple data sources, such as location data needed for a ridesharing app.

8. Mitigate the risks of bots or malicious actors from taking advantage of compensation for access to data. For example, when Microsoft experimented with paying users for data, bots—with no usable information—exploited the system.[4]

9. Make it easy to move data across platforms, without expecting the user to be a technology expert.

10. Anticipate unintended consequences of changes as fundamental as transferring the control and management of data from Big Tech "professionals" to the "regular" users.

As the multiplicity of solutions and this checklist suggests, finding a workable digital agency solution is daunting. While users are not abandoning digital platforms, they are the proverbial frogs in steadily warming water. Company leaders, pundits, and politicians fuel the fire with rhetoric, but ultimately that's not getting us anywhere. It is time to give users more rights of digital agency and figure out which parts of the data checklist are most practical, scalable, and sustainable. If consumers help demand it, we can find forward-looking solutions that draw upon the wealth of ideas on the table before the water boils over.

Despite feeling a high level of concern about how their data is used, most users continue to hand over their data and tick consent boxes. This "privacy paradox," where users' concerns aren't reflected in their behaviors, points to a flawed system.

✓ Companies and regulators need to move toward a consensus that defines and grants users *digital agency*—the ability for individuals to own the rights to their personal data, manage access to this data, and potentially be compensated fairly for such access.

✓ A number of possible ways to give users direct ownership of their data have been proposed by legislators as well as Big Tech companies themselves. Some comprehensive measures, including the European Union's GDPR and the California Consumer Privacy Act, are now being implemented.

✓ Any workable solution to data governance would need to manage a list of requirements that includes creating a transparent, market-based valuation of personal data, defining standards for how data is stored, and making it easy to move data across platforms.

NOTES

1. Kim Hart, "Consumers Kinda, Sorta Care About Their Data," axios.com, February 25, 2019, https://www.axios.com/consumers -kinda-sorta-care-about-their-data-3292eae9-2176-4a12-b8b5 -8f2de4311907.html.

2. Brooke Auxier, Lee Rainie, Monica Anderson, Andrew Perrin, Madhu Kumar, and Erica Turner, "Americans' Attitudes and Experiences with Privacy Policies and Laws," Pew Research Center, November 15, 2019, https://www.pewresearch.org/internet/2019 /11/15/americans-attitudes-and-experiences-with-privacy-policies -and-laws/.

3. Luc Rocher, Julien M. Hendrickx, and Yves-Alexandre de Montjoye, "Estimating the Success of Re-identifications in Incomplete Datasets Using Generative Models," *Nature Communications* 10 (2019), https://www.nature.com/articles/s41467-019-10933-3.

4. Courtney Goldsmith, "Nothing Personal: The Importance of Creating Data Ownership Frameworks," *European CEO*, March 18, 2019, https://www.europeanceo.com/industry-outlook /nothing-personal-the-importance-of-creating-data-ownership -frameworks/.

Adapted from "Why It's So Hard for Users to Control Their Data," on hbr.org, January 30, 2020 (product #H05DVB).

11

HOW TO SAFEGUARD AGAINST CYBERATTACKS ON UTILITIES

by Stuart Madnick

I n the fall of 2019, in Northern California, the United States experienced its first-ever long-lasting and deliberate, large-scale blackout. Fueled by increased fears of devastating fires due to its century-old equipment, the region's utility companies shut off power to more than 1.5 million people, forcing many evacuations. The impact was devastating; Michael Wara, a climate and energy expert at

Stanford University, estimated the cost to California as up to $2.5 billion. For cybersecurity experts like myself, the blackout was a signal of just how precarious our reliance on electricity is, and how much we have to fear in cyberattacks.

Think about what would happen if a cyberattack brought down the power grid in New York or even just a larger part of the country. As we saw in California, people could manage for a few hours—maybe a few days—but what would happen if the outage lasted for a week or more? If a utility in a high-density population area was targeted with a cyberattack, is an evacuation of millions of people feasible or desirable?

Questions we should all be asking include: What do we do if the power grid is breached, making electric-start backup generators unusable? What's the backup plan for the backup plan? What happens to our food supply? Our water supply? Our sewer systems? Our financial systems? Our economy? Answering these questions requires systems-level thinking about how everything is connected and consideration of the interdependencies. For example, hospitals might have backup generators. But what about the supply line for refueling? If the refueling stations need electricity to operate pumps, what is the plan?

Acknowledgment: This research was supported, in part, by funds from the members of the Cybersecurity at MIT Sloan (CAMS) consortium.

Planning for the Unexpected

We all understand that there are certain catastrophes that can reoccur, such as hurricanes or wildfires. But how do you prepare for a catastrophe that has never occurred before? We do not do well at addressing things that we have never seen before.

Consider what happened in 2017 when an area of Wyoming was hit by a strong windstorm that knocked down many large power lines. It took about a week to restore power due to heavy snow and frozen ground. Initially, water and sewage treatment continued due to backup generators. But the pumps that moved sewage from low-lying areas to the treatment plants on higher ground were not designed to have generators, since they could hold several days of waste. After three days with no power, they started backing up. The water then had to be cut off to prevent backed-up wastewater from getting into homes, and the town had to be evacuated. As a spokesperson for the Jackson Hole Mountain Resort said: "This will probably be the longest time that we have had to close . . . in our history." No one had anticipated such a scenario or sequence of events.

The Wyoming windstorm and the California fire threats provide cybersecurity researchers with real-life tests of what to expect when we don't know what could happen. We haven't faced a large-scale cyberattack. Based on conversations I have had with experts in the field, we are as unprepared for a major cyberattack as Wyoming was for the windstorm and California for the fire threat, regardless of whether you're talking about the regional or city level, or the private sector. As Professor Lawrence Susskind, in MIT's urban systems department, described it to me, "[In a cyberattack today] millions [of people] . . . could be left with no electricity, no water, no public transportation, and no waste disposal for weeks (or even months)."

Weeks and months, as it happens, are good estimates for how long it could take to come back online after an attack on a utility. A cyberattack can disrupt a traditional computer system by manipulating the software or erasing data, but the physical computer is still intact, and with various degrees of effort, the software and data can be restored. But a cyberphysical system, such as a generator or similar computer-control equipment, can be destroyed—that is, made to explode. Repairing or replacing such systems can take weeks or even months, especially if many are destroyed at the same time, since spare systems and parts are usually scarce and often custom manufactured.

Evaluating Our Risk

Some have asked me why such a major cyberattack of this nature hasn't already occurred. I believe there are three necessary conditions for one to happen: opportunity, capability, and motivation.

Opportunity: Too often factories and energy companies believe that if they are not directly connected to the internet, they are safe from attack. This is not the case. There are plenty of ways to "jump" that gap to launch a cyberattack, as the Iranians learned when their uranium enrichment facility was attacked by the computer worm Stuxnet. Relying on this method of "protection" has created opportunities and openings for attacks around the world.

Capability: Given that there may be ways to "get in," do the attackers have the capability to do damage? There is also plenty of capability out there. Although much attention has focused on the major state actors, such as China, Russia, North Korea, and Iran, the reality is that an attacker does not need billions of dollars or thousands of people. As I sometimes say, "The good guys are getting better, but the bad guys are getting badder faster." The tools to accomplish attacks are increasingly available on the Dark Web at decreasing costs, including cyber-weapons stolen from NSA and the CIA. For example, the Ukraine power grid attack used spear phishing, in-dustrial control, and disk-wiping techniques that were all readily available on the black market, many of them previously stolen from NSA.

Motivation: So far, motivation has been our major saving grace. What does the attacker gain by shutting down the power grid of another country? In the case of kinetic war-fare (such as a missile attack), the possibility of retaliation acts as a strong deterrent. Satellites easily spot the origin of the missile, and retaliation is likely to soon follow. But those checks and balances do not work as well for cyber-warfare where plausible deniability—or even misdirect-ing the blame to someone else—is so easy. As the *New York Times* recently reported, "Groups linked to Russia's intelligence agencies [. . .] had recently been uncovered boring into the network of an elite Iranian hacking unit and attacking governments and private companies in the Middle East and Britain—hoping Tehran would be blamed for the havoc."[1] Relying on the lack of motiva-tion and luck is not a safe way going forward.

How to Better Prepare

There are at least three problems with the way we have addressed such issues in the past that need to change:

Driving forward by looking through the rearview mirror: This is an old cliché but very appropriate. We usually focus our future actions in response to the last cyberattack. Although that helps prevent future reoccurrences, which is good, it does little to address the cyberattack that we have never seen before. In some bizarre cases, the attackers actually took advantage of what they knew their target had done to respond to their last cyberattack to make their next cyberattack even more effective. There needs to be visionary thinking: not just what *has* happened, but what *could* happen.

Getting overwhelmed by addressing the causes rather than the impacts: In trying to think about and prepare for new cyberattacks, we often start by thinking about how the cyberattack might originate. Instead, we should focus on what we can do to minimize the damage. Our cybersafety analysis method, developed with my colleague Shaharyar Khan, starts with a focus on what we are trying to prevent, and then what controls or facilities can minimize the possibility of that outcome. For example, as part of a cybersafety analysis of a company's central utility system, our team determined that a relatively inexpensive relay costing about $6,000 could safeguard against a cyberattack targeting the automatic voltage regulator (AVR) of a generator. This upgrade would prevent $11 million worth of direct damage to the generator in addition to preventing subsequent outage damage of the cost of repairs and lost revenue. Of course, if many such generators were targeted at the same time, the resulting widespread power outage would be substantial and long term.

Not considering overlooked interdependencies and the unique properties of cyberphysical systems: Based on our past experiences, most people, especially engineers working with physical systems, assume independent failures. That is, there is of course some chance that generator #1, which is a mechanical device, will fail at some point. But it is unlikely that generator #2 will fail at the same time, and extremely unlikely that generators #1, #2, and #3 will fail at the same time, etc. Considering the physical properties, those assumptions are reasonable. But a cyberattack that destroys generator #1 can just as easily destroy all the others at the same time. Our emergency preparedness needs to not only take this into account but also plan for it.

What We Risk by Not Imagining the Unknown

To illustrate the risks we face by not planning, consider again the California blackouts of 2019; 248 hospitals were in regions that lost power. "I can't overemphasize the calamity that these events cause at the neighborhood level. Hundreds of health-care facilities don't have backup generators," said Jack Brouwer, an engineering professor and director of the National Fuel Cell Research Center at the University of California, Irvine. Referencing the deaths caused by previous wildfires in California, he said, "If you're out of power for an hour, that's fine, but for a couple of days—those lives count as much as those that would be lost in a fire."

It's time to imagine the unimaginable, and the California power outages have provided us with a small glimpse of what could happen if we don't prepare. As we face increasingly global uncertainty and insecurity, we need more innovative and systems-level thinking—and a sense of urgency to mitigate the impact of a major cyberattack before it happens.

TAKEAWAYS

Our approach to cybersecurity must evolve to anticipate types of attacks we've never seen before—such as an attack on the power grid of a major metropolitan area. Recent disasters provide us a glimpse of what the unimaginable could be and show us how necessary it is to safeguard against it. There are at least three behaviors we need to change:

✓ Driving forward by looking through the rearview mirror: Responding to the last cyberattack can help prevent future reoccurrences but does little to address an attack we've never seen before. Visionary thinking is needed.

✓ Getting overwhelmed by addressing the causes rather than the impacts: Instead of focusing on how an attack might originate, we should concentrate on what we can do to minimize the damage that attacks cause.

✓ Overlooking interdependencies and the unique properties of cyberphysical systems: Under normal circumstances redundant mechanical systems will break down at different times—but a cyber-attack could cause a system and all its backups to fail simultaneously.

NOTE

1. Matthew Rosenberg, Nicole Perlroth, and David E. Sanger, "'Chaos Is the Point': Russian Hackers and Trolls Grow Stealthier in 2020," *New York Times*, January 10, 2020, https://www.nytimes .com/2020/01/10/us/politics/russia-hacking-disinformation -election.html.

Adapted from "How to Safeguard Against Cyberattacks on Utilities," on hbr.org, January 23, 2020 (product #H05DAL).

12

A SURVIVAL GUIDE FOR STARTUPS IN THE ERA OF TECH GIANTS

by Thales S. Teixeira

S tartups and established companies all face a di-
lemma when building new technology products. If
they hit upon something innovative that has high
potential, they invite the scrutiny of large technology
companies such as Amazon, Google, Facebook, and Microsoft. Big Tech has the money, technology, data, and
talent to replicate and enhance any technological innovation that is not fully protected by patents—which encompasses most digital products.

Recent episodes have shown this copycat behavior to be quite common and life-threatening to startups. The copying comes in various flavors. Sometimes tech giants simply copy innovative features. When Snapchat was doing well with stories that disappeared after 24 hours, for example, Facebook retaliated by introducing the same feature to its products, including Instagram and WhatsApp. Subsequently, Snapchat's usership stalled. It has had trouble regaining momentum, and its stock price went down dramatically.

In more egregious cases, whole "form factors" (in Silicon Valley jargon) have been copied. After years of growing its user base at nearly 5% per month (!), Slack's adoption rate has slackened and started to show signs of decline. The pivotal event? The introduction of Microsoft's knockoff product, Teams. Microsoft did what it does best: waited to see signs of success (four years, in this case), then copied the offering and later integrated it into its other products.

A third approach is to copy a niche product. Allbirds acquired a cult following by developing a line of wool shoes sourced in an environmentally responsible manner. In response, Amazon copied the top-selling product almost point-for-point and sold it online for nearly half the price.

Acknowledgment: Leandro Guissoni, Mark Hill, Greg Piechota, and Hem Suri provided valuable suggestions for this article.

Despite this predatory behavior—and the resulting reluctance of some venture capitalists to invest—a few startups have managed to survive beyond their early stages and become sizable players in the same space as the tech giants. On the surface, it looks as if they succeeded due to luck or lack of interest on Big Tech's part. In reality, though, these challengers succeeded by using the companies' strengths against them. This strategic move, although counterintuitive at first, can lead to copy-proof innovation.

Consider Wayfair. Today it's the largest online seller of home goods and furniture. Back in 2014, a Harvard case I coauthored described how the company had just merged more than two hundred niche product websites into the Wayfair brand. When I spoke with its cofounder and CEO, Niraj Shah, it was clear that Amazon was the constant threat. Over the years, Wayfair had implemented many features that it had seen work for Amazon, and Amazon developers also copied features from Wayfair.

One thing that Amazon did not replicate—and that worked remarkably well for Wayfair—was taking its own pictures of and measurements for the furniture and home furnishings that it sold. This additional detail helped consumers visualize the home decor they were planning, and it helped Wayfair to differentiate itself and get traction. (Its five-year revenue growth has been an astounding 49%

[CAGR], compared to Amazon's 26%.) Yet Amazon continued to show only the pictures provided by the manufacturer.

Why? I suspect it's because Amazon has 3 billion items for sale, whereas Wayfair offers 14 million. The infrastructure and added cost that Amazon would require to take unique pictures of products is daunting, particularly given that more than half its sales comes from the marketplace listings that are managed independently by third-party sellers. And it's not just about costs. To succeed with Wayfair's approach, Amazon would need longer lead times for adding new products, reducing the speed of growth at the "everything store." Plus, it would cause the website to load slower and be more visually cluttered. Amazon could have copied Wayfair, but it chose not to, as that was not in its own interest.

Zulily, which sells women's and children's clothing online, found another approach to competing with Amazon in a way that the giant retailer chose not to emulate. Amazon is relentlessly customer-centric: Shoppers tend to get lower prices, quicker delivery times, and great customer service. However, in retailing, catering to the shopper above all else comes at the expense of the supplier—and Amazon's suppliers put up with a lot. Amazon routinely withholds or delays payment, often arbitrarily. Worse, it copies suppliers' products and undercuts them, often putting the supplier out of business.

So it made perfect sense for Zulily to offer suppliers high-quality service, commit to volume purchases, and offer fair purchase prices. As a result of Zulily's approach, many suppliers accepted exclusive supply deals with the startup instead of selling on Amazon's much larger marketplace. This, in turn, allowed Zulily to offer novel and unique items not available elsewhere. The company grew revenues tremendously—from 2009 to 2014 at a CAGR of 161%—until it was acquired by Qurate, owners of QVC and HSN, in 2015 for $2.4 billion as this Harvard case study shows.

Outside of e-commerce, in its early days Dropbox took advantage of Microsoft's massive enterprise software sales prowess. For years, Dropbox was a tiny startup with only a few dozen employees and no salesforce to sell cloud storage to enterprise CIOs and CTOs. Instead, Dropbox offers its service for free to individual consumers. As people adopted the service and it grew, Dropbox got this network of people to start using its product at work. Over time, those users lobbied their bosses, CIOs and CTOs, to purchase and offer Dropbox Business, the subject of a Harvard case study. In other words, they used personal consumption as a Trojan horse.

This judo-like approach, in which a smaller challenger leverages the opponent's larger size and strength, is promising, but it's certainly not guaranteed to work or to be sustainable over the long haul. If they don't copy you, the giant you're challenging might opt to build a stand-alone competitor and still copy point-for-point what you built. That said, it's generally easier to compete with a stand-alone spin-off than the "mother ship." When TikTok offered a video-sharing app that allowed users to share music snippets, it appealed to younger users who thought Facebook was for their parents and grandparents, and it quickly grained traction. In response, Facebook launched a nearly identical stand-alone app called Lasso, which thus far has not gained traction.

Alternatively, Big Tech might simply attempt to acquire the threat. But that's not guaranteed to succeed either. Acquisition is sometimes very costly, and increasingly, it's just not an option. Facebook did try to buy Snapchat and was denied. Microsoft did try to buy Slack without success. In these cases, it was the startup founders and investors who rejected the offers. Amazon, reputationally the least acquisition prone of the Big Tech bunch, has historically preferred to develop in-house rather than acquire from outside.

I have been using this approach with the startups that I advise to various degrees of success. In order to leverage Big Tech's strengths against them and avoid being besieged by copycat behavior, you will need to address these questions:

1. Does the opponent have *a major strength* that is predominantly responsible for its success?

2. Can you identify a product offering (niche, feature, or format) that a segment of customers value and the delivery of which is made harder by possessing the above-mentioned strength?

3. Would mimicking the novel offering somehow hurt the larger opponent's main business?

4. If the product offering eventually has traction in the market, would the Big Tech opponent necessarily need to give up its strength to copy or compete?

If you can answer yes to these questions, then you too may have found a way to deter blatant copying and to succeed unencumbered. Of course, no single strategy can deliver an advantage forever. In order to thrive, constantly creating copy-proof innovation is essential.

TAKEAWAYS

Many startups challenge tech giants like Facebook and Amazon, but few succeed, in part because digital titans easily and effectively copy technological innovation. But there are ways to use Big Tech's size and strengths against them. To avoid being besieged by copycat behavior, address these questions:

1. Does the opponent have *a major strength* that is predominantly responsible for its success?

2. Can you identify a product offering (niche, feature, or format) that a segment of customers value and the delivery of which is made harder by possessing the above-mentioned strength?

3. Would mimicking the novel offering somehow hurt the larger opponent's main business?

4. If the product offering eventually has traction in the market, would the Big Tech opponent necessarily need to give up its strength to copy or compete?

Adapted from "A Survival Guide for Startups in the Era of Tech Giants," on hbr.org, October 1, 2019 (product #H05FT9).

About the Contributors

OMAR ABBOSH is Group Chief Executive of Accenture's Communications, Media & Technology operating group and coauthor of *Pivot to the Future: Discovering Value and Creating Growth in a Disrupted World*.

MATT BEANE is an assistant professor of technology management at the University of California, Santa Barbara, and a research affiliate with MIT's Initiative on the Digital Economy.

BHASKAR CHAKRAVORTI is the Dean of Global Business at The Fletcher School at Tufts University and founding Executive Director of Fletcher's Institute for Business in the Global Context. He is the author of *The Slow Pace of Fast Change*.

TOMAS CHAMORRO-PREMUZIC is the Chief Talent Scientist at ManpowerGroup, a professor of business psychology at University College London and at Columbia University, and an associate at Harvard's Entrepreneurial Finance

Lab. He is the author of *Why Do So Many Incompetent Men Become Leaders? (and How to Fix It)* (Harvard Business Review Press, 2019). Follow him on Twitter @drtcp.

BEN DATTNER is an executive coach and organizational development consultant and the founder of New York City–based Dattner Consulting, LLC. Follow him on Twitter @bendattner.

LARRY DOWNES is a coauthor of *Pivot to the Future: Discovering Value and Creating Growth in a Disrupted World*. His earlier books include *Big Bang Disruption*, *The Laws of Disruption*, and *Unleashing the Killer App*.

DAVID FURLONGER is a vice president at Gartner and a Gartner Research Fellow. He is coauthor of *The Real Business of Blockchain: How Leaders Can Create Value in a New Digital Age* (Harvard Business Review Press, 2019).

MATTHEW GILLESPIE is a creative project manager at Fractl, where he oversees content marketing campaigns rooted in behavioral research and large data set analysis.

ASIT GOEL is a partner in the San Francisco office of Bain & Company. He is a leader in the firm's global technology practice.

LAUREN GOLEMBIEWSKI is CEO and cofounder of Voxable, an agency that designs and develops chatbots and voice interfaces. She advises companies ranging from the *Fortune* 10 to startups about how they can most effectively leverage AI to communicate and empower their customers and employees.

JACOB L. H. JONES is the Creative Process Engineer at Fractl and heads the consumer research initiatives out of Fractl's Denver office.

KELSEY LIBERT is a viral marketing speaker and Director of Promotions at Fractl. Follow her on Twitter @KelseyLibert.

STUART MADNICK is the John Norris Maguire (1960) Professor of Information Technologies in the MIT Sloan School of Management, Professor of Engineering Systems in the MIT School of Engineering, and Director of Cybersecurity at MIT Sloan (CAMS): the Interdisciplinary Consortium for Improving Critical Infrastructure Cybersecurity. He has been active in the cybersecurity field since coauthoring the book *Computer Security* in 1979.

FRIDA POLLI, a cognitive neuroscientist, is the cofounder and CEO of pymetrics, a platform that uses behavioral science and AI to match people to jobs accurately and fairly.

DARRELL K. RIGBY is a partner in the Boston office of Bain & Company. He heads the firm's global innovation practice. He is the author of *Doing Agile Right: Transformation Without Chaos* (Harvard Business Review Press, 2020).

KANE SIMMS is the Founder of VUX World, an industry-leading podcast and voice-design studio helping brands, agencies, and individuals create world-class voice experiences. Kane is a thought leader in the voice industry and is a frequent speaker and host at voice events and conferences.

THALES S. TEIXEIRA is the cofounder of Decoupling.co, a digital disruption and transformation consulting firm. Previously he was a professor at Harvard Business School for ten years. He is the author of *Unlocking the Customer Value Chain: How Decoupling Drives Consumer Disruption.*

CHRISTOPHE UZUREAU is a vice president at Gartner. He is co-author of *The Real Business of Blockchain: How Leaders Can Create Value in a New Digital Age* (Harvard Business Review Press, 2019).

MIKEY VU is a partner in the Chicago office of Bain & Company. He is a leader in the firm's Retail and Digital practices.

DAVID WEINBERGER is a senior researcher at Harvard's Berkman Klein Center for Internet & Society and the author, most recently, of *Everyday Chaos* (Harvard Business Review Press, 2019).

SARA WILSON is a brand and digital content strategist who helps brands, publishers, and influencers find, engage, and build their audiences across digital channels. As the founder and principal of SW Projects, she has advised brands including Bumble, the *New York Times*, *National Geographic*, Sony Pictures Television, *Bustle*, *Playboy*, and others. Prior to founding SW Projects, she oversaw lifestyle partnerships at Facebook and Instagram.

Index

Is Your Business Ready for the Future?

If you enjoyed this book and want more on today's pressing business topics, turn to other books in the **Insights You Need** series from *Harvard Business Review*. Featuring HBR's latest thinking on topics critical to your company's success—from Blockchain and Cybersecurity to AI and Agile—each book will help you explore these trends and how they will impact you and your business in the future.

Engage with HBR content the way you want, on any device.

With HBR's new subscription plans, you can access world-renowned **case studies** from Harvard Business School and receive **four free eBooks**. Download and customize prebuilt **slide decks and graphics** from our **Visual Library**. With HBR's archive, top 50 best-selling articles, and five new articles every day, HBR is more than just a magazine.

Subscribe Today
hbr.org/success